First World War
and Army of Occupation
War Diary
France, Belgium and Germany

60 DIVISION
Divisional Troops
2/4 London Field Company Royal Engineers
1 December 1915 - 30 November 1916

WO95/3028/2

The Naval & Military Press Ltd
www.nmarchive.com
Published in association with The National Archives

Published by

The Naval & Military Press Ltd

Unit 10 Ridgewood Industrial Park,

Uckfield, East Sussex,

TN22 5QE England

Tel: +44 (0) 1825 749494

www.naval-military-press.com

www.nmarchive.com

This diary has been reprinted in facsimile from the original. Any imperfections are inevitably reproduced and the quality may fall short of modern type and cartographic standards.

© **Crown Copyright**
Images reproduced by permission of The National Archives, London, England, 2015.

Contents

Document type	Place/Title	Date From	Date To
Heading	WO95/3028/2		
Heading	2-4th London Fld Coy R.E. 1915 Aug 1916 Nov		
Heading	1/4 London Fd Coy Reg. Vol IX X & XI		
Miscellaneous	60th (London) Divisional Engineers	04/09/1915	04/09/1915
Heading	2/4th Field Company RE T 60th (London) Division From December 1st 1915 To December 31st 1915		
War Diary	Stortford	01/12/1915	31/12/1915
War Diary	Sutton Veny	01/03/1916	31/03/1916
Heading	War Diary Of 2/4th Field Company R.E.T. 60th London Division From April 1st To April 30th 1916		
War Diary	Sutton Veny	01/04/1916	30/04/1916
Miscellaneous	2/4th Field Company RE Programme Of Traning Sappers	30/03/1916	30/03/1916
War Diary	Sutton Veny	01/05/1916	31/05/1916
Miscellaneous	2/4th Field Company R.E (Programme And Training)	06/05/1916	06/05/1916
Miscellaneous	2/4th Field Company R.E.T (Programme And Training)	13/05/1916	13/05/1916
Miscellaneous	2/4th Field Company R.E (Programme Of Training)	20/05/1916	20/05/1916
Miscellaneous	2/4th Field Company R.E (Programme Of Training)	27/05/1916	27/05/1916
War Diary	Sutton Veny	01/06/1916	22/06/1916
Miscellaneous	Appendix A 2/4th Field Company. R.E.	03/06/1916	03/06/1916
Miscellaneous	Appendix B Company. R.E.	19/06/1916	19/06/1916
War Diary	Sutton Veny	22/06/1916	22/06/1916
War Diary	Southampton	22/06/1916	22/06/1916
War Diary	Havre	23/06/1916	24/06/1916
War Diary	St. Pol	25/06/1916	25/06/1916
War Diary	Penin	26/06/1916	26/06/1916
War Diary	Maroeuil	28/06/1916	30/06/1916
Miscellaneous	Appendix D 2/4th Field Co. R.E.	24/06/1916	24/06/1916
Miscellaneous	Appendix C 2/4th Field Co. R.E.	17/06/1916	17/06/1916
War Diary	Maroeuil	01/07/1916	06/07/1916
War Diary	Left Of Douai	07/07/1916	07/07/1916
War Diary	Baird Street	10/07/1916	10/07/1916
War Diary	Support Pt Pulpit	10/07/1916	10/07/1916
War Diary	Maroeuil	11/07/1916	11/07/1916
War Diary	Zivy	12/07/1916	12/07/1916
War Diary	Mercier	12/07/1916	12/07/1916
War Diary	Bentata Redt	12/07/1916	12/07/1916
War Diary	Maroeuil	12/07/1916	12/07/1916
War Diary	Bau-Des-Abris	12/07/1916	12/07/1916
War Diary	Rocade Avenue	12/07/1916	12/07/1916
War Diary	Claudot	12/07/1916	12/07/1916
War Diary	Labyrinth Redt	12/07/1916	12/07/1916
War Diary	Maroeuil	13/07/1916	13/07/1916
War Diary	Mercier	13/07/1916	13/07/1916
War Diary	Maroeuil	14/07/1916	18/07/1916
War Diary	Claudot	19/07/1916	19/07/1916
War Diary	Maroeuil	20/07/1916	25/07/1916
War Diary	Vase	26/07/1916	26/07/1916
War Diary	Maroeuil	27/07/1916	29/07/1916
War Diary	Territorial Av Maroeuil	29/07/1916	29/07/1916

War Diary	Bessant Claudot Junc	31/07/1916	31/07/1916
War Diary	Firing Line	31/07/1916	31/07/1916
War Diary	Re Shelters	31/07/1916	31/07/1916
War Diary	Nr Glasgow Dump	31/07/1916	31/07/1916
War Diary	Bessant	31/07/1916	31/07/1916
Heading	War Diary 2/4th London Field Coy R.E.		
War Diary	Maroeuil	01/08/1916	31/08/1916
Heading	War Diary 2/4th London Field Coy R.E. September 1916		
War Diary	Maroeuil	31/08/1916	30/09/1916
Heading	War Diary 2/4th London Field Coy R.E. October 1916		
War Diary	Maroeuil	01/10/1916	24/10/1916
War Diary	Ferme Doffine	25/10/1916	25/10/1916
War Diary	Buneville	26/10/1916	28/10/1916
War Diary	Wavans	29/10/1916	29/10/1916
War Diary	Prouville	30/10/1916	30/10/1916
War Diary	Toutencourt	31/10/1916	31/10/1916
Heading	War Diary 2/4th London Field Coy R.E. November 1916		
War Diary	Toutencourt	01/11/1916	01/11/1916
War Diary	Prouville	02/11/1916	03/11/1916
War Diary	Eaucourt	04/11/1916	14/11/1916
War Diary	Longpre	15/11/1916	16/11/1916
War Diary	Marseilles	17/11/1916	17/11/1916
War Diary	Carcasson Camp	18/11/1916	19/11/1916
War Diary	H M T Transylvania	20/11/1916	22/11/1916
War Diary	Marseilles	22/11/1916	22/11/1916
War Diary	H M T. Transylvania	23/11/1916	30/11/1916

WO 95/3028/2

60TH DIVISION

2-4TH LONDON FLD COY R.E.

1915 AUG — 1916 NOV

TO SALONIKA
RE NUMBERED 521 (1917 FEB)

47

1/4 London Fd Coy
R.E.

Vol IX
X &
XI

60th (LONDON) DIVISIONAL ENGINEERS.

Notes on War Diary, August, 1915.

UNIT.	2/4th LONDON FIELD COY. R.E. 60th (London) Divsl. Engineers.
Mobilization Centre.	Duke of York's Headquarters, Chelsea.

Stations since occupied subsequent to Concentration:-

    Chelsea, London.
    Nutfield, Surrey.
    Radlett, Herts.
    Brightlingsea, Essex.
    Harlow, Essex.
    Stansted, Essex.

Temporary War Station.   Stansted, Essex.

UNIT.	3/3rd LONDON FIELD COY. R.E. 60th (London) Divsl. Engineers.
Mobilization Centre.	Duke of York's Headquarters, Chelsea.

Stations since occupied:-
    Chelsea, London.
    Batlers Green, Aldenham, near Watford.
    Stisted, near Braintree.
    Hatfield Broad Oak.
    Brightlingsea, Essex.
    Stansted, Essex.

TRAINING.

The training of both Companies as a whole has been much interfered with by the preparation of Camps for various Units of the Division. The Companies, however have received considerable instruction and practice in Earthworks and Mining, and good progress has been made by the mounted men in riding and driving drill.

The Companies have also made progress in Musketry.

The Companies suffer from a lack of technical and other vehicles, especially the 3/3rd London Field Coy. R.E.

During the month, both Companies have moved under canvas.

[signature: Ralph A...]

Lieut.-Colonel, R.E.T.
C.R.E.
60th (London) Division.

Weston House,
Stansted, Essex.
4th Septr. 1915.

C O N F I D E N T I A L

WAR DIARY.
of the
2/4th Field Company R.E.T. 60th(London)Division.
From December 1st 1915.   To December 31st 1915.

VOLUME, 1.

Army form C. 2118. Page 1.

WAR DIARY for December.

UNIT. 2/4th Field Company. 60th London Division. STATION. Bishops Stortford Herts. DATE. January 3rd 1916.

Hour	Date	Place	Summary of events and information.	Remarks and references to Appendices.
A.M. P.M. 8-30 TO 4-0	1/12/15	Bps Stortford	Trained Men. Brushwood Huts. MESSING FIELD. Physical & Squad Drill Lecture on outposts, Recruits. Musketry triangle of error. MESSING FIELD.	all References are on O.S. SHEET No 29, ½"to1 MILE.
8-30 to 11-0am	2/12/15	"	Trained Men. Check parade & Foot inspection MESSING FIELD. Night Revetting, AISA LODGE.	
12" to 8-30 to 4-0pm	"	"	Recruits. Blocks & Tackles, Splicing, Knotting & Lashing, MESSING FIELD.	
8-30 to 4-0	3/12/15	"	Trained Men. Check parade & Lecture on obstacles. MESSING FIELD Physical & Squad Drill Recapitulation, Lecture on Recruits. Obstacles. MESSING FIELD. Officers. Reconnaissance of BISHOPS STORTFORD RAILWAY STATION.	
8-30 to12-0	4/12/15	"	Trained Men. Physical, Company & Extended order Drill MESSING FIELD. Recruits. Spar Bridging, RIVERSTORT	
9-30	5/12/15	"	Church Parade.	
8-30 to 4-0	6/12/15	"	Trained Men. Demolitions. BURY GREEN. Recruits. Wire entanglements, lecture on explosives & Physical Drill MESSING FIELD.	
8-30 to 4-0	7/12/15	"	Trained Men. Portable wire entanglements, automatic alarms. MESSINGFIELD. Recruits. Route March, FARNHAM, UPWICK GREEN, LITTLE HADHAM, BISHOPS STORTFORD. Reconnaissance of RIVER ASH. Departure. Serjt Elliott L.A.L. 1077. Granted Commission with 3/5th London Brigade R.F.A.	Authority T.F. Records No 3342 R.E. 2. 3/12/15.
" "	8/12/15	"	Trained Men. Brushwood Cutting. BASSINGBOURNE HALL. Recruits. Earthworks & Revetting, AISA LODGE.	

Army form C. 2118. Page 2.

WAR DIARY for December.

UNIT. 2/4th Field Company. 66th London Division. S.W.T.M. Bishops Stortford Herts. DATE. January 3rd 1916.

Hour	Date	Place	Summary of events and information.	Remarks and references to Appendices.
8-30 to 4-0	9/12/15	Bps, Stortford	Trained Men. Brushwood Huts, Hurdles, Gabions. MESSING FIELD. Recruits. Trestle Bridging, Bridging Expedients RIVER STORT.	
"	10/12/15	"	Course. 2nd Lieut Shove Commenced a course of Farriery at WHARF HOUSE.	
"	"	"	Trained Men. Pontoon, Rafts, Bridging. RIVER STORT. Squad & Physical Drill Musketry. MESSING FIELD Recruits. Field Sketching FARNHAM ROAD. Recruits making good progress.	
8-30 to 12-0	11/12/15	"	Trained Men. Company & Extended order Drill MESSING FIELD Recruits. Demolitions. BURY GREEN.	
10-0 am	12/12/15	"	Church Parade.	
8-30 11-0am	13/12/15	"	Trained Men. Kit inspection. MESSING FIELD. Night digging & Revettments AISA LODGE	
8-30 to 4-0	"	"	Recruits. Physical Drill Progressive musketry MESSING FIELD. Visual Training FARNHAM ROAD.	
11pm to 6am 8-30 to 4-0	14/12/15	"	Trained Men. Night obstacles. AISA LODGE. Recruits. Physical Drill MESSING FIELD Improvised Bridges. RIVER STORT.	
3pm to 4pm 8-30 to 4-0	15/12/15	"	Trained Men. Foot inspection. Check parade MESSING FIELD Recruits. Lock Bridging RIVER STORT.	
8-30 to 4-0	16/12/15	"	Trained Men. Route March:- WALLBURY CAMP, WOODSIDE GREEN, HOW-GREEN, GREAT HALLINGBURY, BLUNTS, BIRCHANGER. Recruits. Physical Drill, Straw mats, Thatching, Loading & Unloading Pontoons SILVERLEYS.	
"	"	"	Transfers Corporal Holloway W.T. Transfered to 1/6th Field Coy, R.E. BISHOPS STORTFORD.	

Authority T.F. Records No 3269 R.E. 2. 14/12/15

WAR DIARY for December.

Army Form C. 2118. Page 3.

UNIT. 2/4th Field Company. 60th London Division. STATION. Bishops Stortford Herts. DATE. January 3rd 1916.

Hour	Date	Place	Summary of events and information.	Remarks and references to Appendices.
8-30 to 4-0	17/12/15	Bps Stortford	Trained Men. Completion of Brushwood Huts, Mousing, Seizing? & Whipping. Water Supply, Pumps, Troughs. MESSING FIELD.	*sig*
"	"	"	Recruits. Route March:- HAZEL END, HASSOBURY, BENTFIELD END STANSTED. Road Reconnaissance FARNHAM AND HAZEL END.(no sore Feet)	*sig*
8-30 to 12-0	18/12/15	"	Trained Men. Squad, Company, & extended order Drill, Saluting MESSING FIELD	*sig*
"	"	"	Recruits Entanglements & automatic alarms MESSING FIELD.	*sig*
9-30	19/12/15	"	Church Parade.	*sig*
8-30 to 1-0	20/12/15	"	Trained Men. Visual Training & Ranging, use of Mekometer, taking angles & use of Clinometer. BURY GREEN. Physical Drill, Camping arrangements troughs,	*sig*
"	"	"	Recruits & Pumps. MESSING FIELD.	*sig*
8-30 to 4-0	"	"	Company Night operations Field works ALSA LODGE.	*sig*
8-30 to 4-0	21/12/15	"	Trained Men. Pontoon & Trestle Bridging. Field oberservations. cordage, and use of spars, swinging derricks. RIVER STORT.	*sig*
"	"	"	Recruits. Brushwood cutting. BERRY LODGE.	*sig*
"	22/12/15	"	Trained Men Pontoon Bridging & Trestle Bridging RIVERSTORT. Brushwood, wire Screens, fascines, gabions, &	
"	"	"	Recruits Hurdles. MESSING FIELD.	*sig*
8-30 to 1-0	23/12/15	"	Trained Men. Bombing MESSING FIELD. Night operations Revetting & obstacles.ALSA LODGE	
8-30 to 4-0	"	"	Recruits. Physical & Progressive Musketry MESSING FIELD	*sig*
"	"	"	Officers. 2nd Lieut Perkins commenced Trench Fighting school course at Kelvedon	

This entry should appear under yesterday's date

Authority (London Divnsl orders No 354 Part 1 Para 1 December 18th 1915.

Army Form C. 2118.

WAR DIARY for December.

UNIT. 2/4th Field Company. 60th London Division. STATION. Bishops Stortford Herts. DATE. January 3rd 1916.

Hour	Date	Place	Summary of events and information.	Remarks and references to Appendices.
7-45	24/12/15	Bps, Stortford	Company Inspection. by Major General Bulfin C.V.O. C.B. commanding 60th London Division, at MAPLE AVENUE.	
	25/12/15	"	2nd Lieut Brown A.O. Discharged from Hospital. 2nd Lieut Turner C.H. Returned from Engineering Course at 2nd Lieut Lane P. Brightlingsea.	
9-30	26/12/15	"	Church Parade. Officers. 2nd Lieut Turner commenced duties as Billeting Officer for Divnsl, Engineers, in Lieu of Lieut Dunnage.	
9-0	27/12/15	"	Company. Check Parade. MESSING FIELD.	
8-30 to 4-0	28/12/15	"	Trained Men. Brushwood cutting BERRY LODGE. Lecture Strength of Materials MESSING FIELD. Recruits. Bridging Expedients RIVER STORT.	
	"	"	Inspection. Captain Stratton of the Central Force inspected the Messing arrangements. MESSING FIELD. Course. The undermentioned Officers & men commenced course of Musketry at WHARF HOUSE. BISHOPS STORTFORD.	
8-30 to 1-0	29/12/15	"	Trained Men. Brushwood cutting BASSINGBOURNE HALL. Night Revetting. AISA LODGE.	
8-30 to 4-0	"	"	Recruits. Brushwood cutting BASSINGBOURNE HALL. Lecture on duties of Sentries & guard mounting. MESSING FIELD.	
	"	"	Departure. Lieut Col, Henriques Proceeded to General Headquarters British Expeditionary Force FRANCE for duty in the field for a period of three days	Authority W.O. Letter 121/7401 (A.G.4 a) 23/12/15
8-30 to 4-0	30/12/15	"	Trained Men. Route March:- SAWBRIDGEWORTH, HATFIELD HEATH, & Recruits. LITTLE HALLINGBURY, WALLBURY CAMP,	
8-30 to 4-0	31/12/15	"	Trained Men. Roadmaking SILVERLEYS STABLES. Recruits. Physical Drill Musketry MESSING FIELD. Rifles. 20 Rifles received from the 2nd 18th London Irish SAFFRON WALDEN.	

Army form C. 2118.

WAR DIARY for December.

UNIT. 2/4th Field Company. 60th London Division. STATION. Bishops Stortford Herts. DATE. January 3rd 1916.

Date	Hour	Place	Summary of events and information.	Remarks and references to Appendices.

Signature

Captain. R.E.T.
O.C. 2/4th Field Company.
60th (London) Division.

Army Form C. 2118.

UNIT. 2/4th Field Company R.E. 60th (London) Division.

WAR DIARY
of
INTELLIGENCE-SUMMARY.
(Erase heading not required.)

Instructions regarding War Diaries and Intelligence Summaries are contained in F. S. Regs., Part II. and the Staff Manual respectively. Title pages will be prepared in manuscript.

March to May 1916

Place	Date	Hour	Summary of Events and Information	Remarks and references to Appendices
SUTTON VENY.	March 1st	a.m. 8.45 to 4.30	Field works.(Sappers); Musketry Instruction (Drivers). 2nd LIEUT. W.B. PERKINS granted 1 month's sick leave.	60th(Lon.)Divn Egrs.Orders 52
	2nd	do.	Field Works. LIEUT. A.F. WILLIAMS, 2nd LIEUT. A.O. BROWN & 2nd LIEUT. C.G. JONES returned from Course of Military Engineering, BRIGHTLINGSEA.	
	3rd	do.	Field Works.	
	4th	9.0 12.0	Company Training. 2nd LIEUT. P.LANE returned from Course of Instruction in Mounted Duties at ALDERSHOT. 2nd LIEUT. H.G. BUXTON proceeded to do. do. No. 980 Sapper ROBERTS, W.E. transferred to Divsl. Headquarters R.E.	T.F.Records 1083R.E.3.3.15
	5th	10.45	Church Parade.	
	6th	8.45 to 4.30	Field Works. ~~Bombark:Rifles:3:303~~ ~~pyrotechnix~~ 2nd LIEUT. P. LANE detailed to superintend Musketry Instruction of Field·Coys.	
	7th	do.	Field Works. 60 short rifles, .303, received.	
	8th	do.	Field Works. 646 Sapper HARVEY,2C.R., returned from Course of Instruction in Cookery, WEYMOUTH 2nd LIEUT. C.H. TURNER discharged from Hospital. do. granted Sick Leave from 8th to 21st March.	
	9th	do.	Field Works.	
	10th	do.	do.	
	11th	do.	do. 2nd LIEUT. C.G. JONES proceeded on one week's leave. No. 1375 Bugler O'NEILL, M.P., re-mustered as Pioneer.	60th(Lon)Divn Egrs.Orders

Army Form C. 2118.

WAR DIARY
2.
INTELLIGENCE SUMMARY.
(Erase heading not required.)

Instructions regarding War Diaries and Intelligence Summaries are contained in F. S. Regs., Part II. and the Staff Manual respectively. Title pages will be prepared in manuscript.

Place	Date	Hour	Summary of Events and Information	Remarks and references to Appendices
	March	a.m.		
SUTTON VENY.	12th	10.45	Church Parade. No. 1848 Driver SHERRING, S., & No. 3183 Sapper SHREEVE? FR. proceeded to CLACTON-ON-SEA to join 7th Provisional Field Coy. R.E.	T.F.Records 1059B.2 2.3.16
	13th	6.30 to 4.30	Musketry: General Musketry Course	
	14th	do.	do. do. do. do. 2nd LIEUT. C.H. TURNER granted 1 month's Sick Leave from 14th March. No. 2389 Sapper CHASTON, S.F., 2625 Sapper EDGELL? P.W., 2323 Sapper LANE, G., 2611 Driver NEWMAN, G., & 2263 Driver SPITTLE, H.G., reported from 3/2nd London Divsl. Engineers for duty.	C.R.,S.C.,R. S106529(A.3) S.C.104760(Q) 27.3.16.
	15th	6.45 to 4.30	Musketry: General Musketry Course. LIEUT. S.G. KILLINGBACK proceeded to School of Cookery, WESTHAM, WEYMOUTH, for 2 days' Course of Cookery.	S.C. letter C.R. 27.3.16.
	16th	do.	Musketry: General Musketry Course.	
	17th	do.	do. do. do.	
	18th	do	Musketry: General Musketry Course. LIEUT. S.G. KILLINGBACK returned from School of Cookery WESTHAM, WEYMOUTH. No. 980 Sapper ROBERTS, W.E. & 3234 Sapper CLARK, F., returned from a Course of Cold Shoeing at ROMSEY.	
	19th	10.45	Church Parade.	
	20th	8.25 to 4.30	Field Works.	
	21st	do.	do.	
	22nd	do.	do.	
	23rd	do.	do.	

Army Form C. 2118.

WAR DIARY

of

~~INTELLIGENCE SUMMARY~~

(Erase heading not required.)

Instructions regarding War Diaries and Intelligence Summaries are contained in F. S. Regs., Part II. and the Staff Manual respectively. Title pages will be prepared in manuscript.

Place	Date	Hour	Summary of Events and Information	Remarks and references to Appendices
SUTTON VENY.	March.a.m.			
	24th	8.45 to 1.0	Route March. - SUTTON VENY, TYTHERINGTON, HEYTESBURY, BISHOPSTROW, BOREHAM, HENFORDS MARSH BOX HILL, CROCKERTON GREEN, SUTTON VENY.	
	25th	9.0	Company Training.	
	26th	10.45	Church Parade. 2nd LIEUT. H.G. BUXTON returned from Course of Mounted Duties at ALDERSHOT 2nd LIEUT. C.G. JONES proceeded to do. do.	60th(Lon)Divn. Orders220 60th(Lon)Divn. Engr.Orders 74.
	27th	8.45 to 4.30	Field Works. 2nd LIEUT. H.V. SHOVE granted 14 days Sick Leave.	
	28th	do.	Field Works.	
	29th	do.	do.	
	30th	do.	do.	
	31st	do.	do.	

Capt.
O.C. 2/4th Field Coy.R.E.
60th (London) Division.

C O N F I D E N T I A L

War Diary

of

2/4th Field Company R.E.T. 60th London Division.

From April 1st to April 30th 1916.

Volume 2.

Army Form C. 2118.

WAR DIARY
or
INTELLIGENCE SUMMARY.
(Erase heading not required.)

Instructions regarding War Diaries and Intelligence Summaries are contained in F. S. Regs., Part II. and the Staff Manual respectively. Title pages will be prepared in manuscript.

Place	Date	Hour	Summary of Events and Information	Remarks and references to Appendices
Sutton Veny.				
	1.4.16		Foot Inspection, Company Drill.	
	2.4.16		2nd Lieut W.B. PERKINS returned from sick leave.	(Authority, Lon. Divsl. Engnrs, orders No. 52 part 2. para 1. dated 2.3.16.)
			Church parade.	
	3.4.16.		Physical Drill and Training as per Appendix (A)	
	4.4.16		Physical Drill and Training as per Appendix (A)	
			2nd Lieut P. LANE, granted 7 days sick leave from April 4th to 10th (inclusive) Authority, Lon. Div. Engnrs, orders No 81. part 2 para 1.5.4.16.	
	5.4.16.		Practice Emergency Alarm Mounted) 7-15 a.m. reported ready to move at 8-05 a.m.	
			Training as per Appendix (A)	
			2nd Lieut W.B. PERKINS granted 14 days sick leave from 5th ot 18th april(inclusive) Authority Lon, Div Engnrs, orders No.83. part 2 para 3 7.4.16.	
			Received of Overseas Boots 237 pairs	
	6.4.16.		Physical Drill & Rifle Inspection & training as per Appendix (A)	
	7.4.16		Foot Inspection, Physical Drill, and Training as per Appendix.(A)	
			No 1226 Corporal HILDCAME 2/4th Fld, Coy R.E. Transferred to 1/6th Fld, Coy R.E.from the 7.4.16.	Authority:- T.F. Records 1652 R.E. 2. 10.3.16.

Army Form C. 2118.
No. 2.

WAR DIARY
or
INTELLIGENCE SUMMARY.
(Erase heading not required.)

Instructions regarding War Diaries and Intelligence Summaries are contained in F. S. Regs., Part II. and the Staff Manual respectively. Title pages will be prepared in manuscript.

Place	Date	Hour	Summary of Events and Information	Remarks and references to Appendices
	8.4.16.		Bayonet Fighting & Company Drill.	
	9.4.16.		Church parade.	
	10.4.16		Physical Drill and Training as per Appendix (B)	
			2nd Lieut H.V. SHOVE was granted extention of sick leave from the 10th to 12th inst	
	11.4.16.		Physical Drill, Rifle inspection, and Training as per Appendix.(B)	
			Emergency Alarm 7-0 p.m. Reported ready to move at 7-45 p.m.	
	12.4.16		Physical Drill and Training as per Appendix (B)	
	13.4.16		Physical Drill and Training as per Appendix (B)	
			Received 162 Rifles, Short, M.L.E. Mark 3, form Ordnance.	
	14.4.16.		Foot inspection, Physical Drill, and Training as per Appendix. (B)	
	15.4.16.		Physical Drill, Kit inspection,(Mounted) Company Drill and Bayonet Fighting.	
			2nd Lieut A.O. BROWN granted 4 days sick leave from 15th to 18th (no authority)	
			2nd Lieut C.G. JONES returned from a course of Mounted Duties at ALDERSHOT. Authority, Lon. Div. orders No 224 20.4.16.	
	16.4.16.		Church Parade, Kit inspection (Dismounted)	

Army Form C. 2118.

WAR DIARY
or
INTELLIGENCE SUMMARY.
(Erase heading not required.)

Instructions regarding War Diaries and Intelligence Summaries are contained in F. S. Regs., Part II. and the Staff Manual respectively. Title pages will be prepared in manuscript.

Place	Date	Hour	Summary of Events and Information	Remarks and references to Appendices
	17.4.16		Physical Drill and Training as per Appendix. (C)	
	18.4.16		Bayonet Fighting and Training as per Appendix.(C)	
	19.4.16.n		Physical Drill and Training as Appendix (C)	
			2nd Lieut A.O. BROWN and 12 men as Advance party proceeded to CHRISTCHURCH on Pontooning course	
	20.4.16		Physical Drill and Training as per Appendix. (C)	
			57 men Proceeded to CHRISTCHURCH on Pontooning course.	
			2nd Lieut H.G. BUXTON Transferred from 2/4th Fld Coy, to Third Line Cum(t.20th inst Authority Lon, District ord. Ref, C.R.L.D.2. 59333 17.4.16.	
			2nd Lieut W.B. PERKINS granted 14 days sick leave from 18th to 1st prox inclusive. Authority Lon. Dis. Engnrs, orders NO 94. part 2 para 3	
	21.4.16.		Church Parade and Foot Inspection. (Good Friday)	
	22.4.16		Physical and Company Drill.	
	23.4.16		Church Parade.	
	24.4.16		Physical Drill and Training as per Appendix (D)	
			1 Serjt and 2 other ranks proceeded to CHRISTCHURCH on Pontooning course.	

Army Form C. 2118.

WAR DIARY
or
INTELLIGENCE SUMMARY.
(Erase heading not required.)

Instructions regarding War Diaries and Intelligence Summaries are contained in F. S. Regs., Part II. and the Staff Manual respectively. Title pages will be prepared in manuscript.

Place	Date	Hour	Summary of Events and Information	Remarks and references to Appendices
	25.4.16		Check parade & Rifle inspection. Training as per Appendix. (B)	
	26.4.16		Bayonet Fighting nad Training as per Appendix. (C)	
	27.4.16		Bomb Throwing and Camp Fatigues	
	28.4.16		Check parade & Rifle inspection. Camp aftigues Kit inspection (Mounted)	
	29.4.16		Foot inspection Physical Drill, Camp Fatigues	
	30.4.16		Church Parade.	

Captain R.E.T.
O.C. 2/4th Field Company
60th London Division.

2/4TH FIELD COMPANY. R.E.

Programme of Training.

(A) 30/3/16

Sappers.

Programme of Training for week ending April 8th, 1916.

Ref. C.S.122. 1" - 1 mile.

Monday.	7.30. to 8.0.		Physical Drill & Rifle Inspection.	PARADE GROUND.
	8.45. to 4.30.		Entrenchments & Fieldworks. Infantry Instruction Party.	SUTTON VENY FIELD WORKS.
Tuesday. Regimental duty.	do:		do:	do:
Wednesday.	7.30 to 8.0.		Physical Drill & Rifle Inspection.	PARADE GROUND.
	9.0. to 10.0.		Knotting & Lashing.	
	8.45. to 4.30.		Infantry Instruction Party.	SUTTON VENY FIELD WORKS.
	11.0. to 3.30.		Route March	SUTTON VENY, WARMINSTER, CROCKERTON, GREEN, LONGBRIDGE DEVERILL, SUTTON VENY. O.S.122.1".
Thursday.	7.30 to 8.0.		Physical drill & Rifle inspection.	PARADE GROUND
	8.45. to 4.30.		Infantry Instruction party.	FIELD WORKS.
	do:		Pontooning.	LONGLEAT PARK.
Friday. Regimental duty.	7.30 to 8.0.		Physical drill & rifle inspection.	PARADE GROUND.
	9.0. to 10.30.		Entrenchments & Fieldworks.	SUTTON VENY FIELD WORKS.
	9.0. to 4.30.		Infantry Instruction party.	do:
	8.30.p.m. to 12.0.		Entrenchments & Fieldworks.	do:
Saturday.	7.30. to 8.0.		Bayonet fighting	PARADE GROUND
	9.0. to 12.0.		Company drill.	do:

Capt.
O.C. 2/4th Field Co: R.E.

(B)

2/4th FIELD COMPANY, R.E.

Programme of Training.

SAPPERS.

Programme of Training for week ending April 15th, 1916.

Ref. O.S. 122, 1" = 1 mile.

Monday.	7.30	to	8.0 Physical Drill & Rifle Inspection.	PARADE GROUND.
Regtl.	8.45	to	4.30 Field Works.	SUTTON VENY FIELD
Duty.		do.	Infantry Instruction Party.	WORKS.
Tuesday.	7.30	to	8.0 Physical Drill & Rifle Inspection.	PARADE GROUND.
	9.0	to	4.0 Entanglements & Alarms.	SUTTON VENY FIELD
				WORKS.
	8.45	to	4.30 Infantry Instruction Party.	do.
Wednesday.	7.30	to	8.0 Physical Drill & Rifle Inspection.	PARADE GROUND.
	9.0	to	10.15 Knotting & Lashing.	do.
	11.0	to	3.30 Route March.	SUTTON VENY, LONG-BRIDGE DEVERILL, CROCKERTON CROSS, SUTTON VENY.
	8.45	to	4.30 Infantry Instruction Party.	SUTTON VENY FIELD WORKS.
Thursday.	7.30	to	8.0 Physical Drill & Rifle Inspection.	PARADE GROUND.
	8.45	to	4.30 Pontooning.	LONGLEAT PARK.
		do.	Infantry Instruction Party.	SUTTON VENY FIELD WORKS.
Friday.	7.30	to	8.0 Physical Drill & Rifle Inspection.	PARADE GROUND.
	8.45	to	3.30 Spar bridging.	CAMP FIELD.
	8.45	to	4.30 Infantry Instruction Party.	SUTTON VENY FIELD WORKS.
	9.0 p.m. to		11.30 p.m. Entanglements & Alarms.	do.
Saturday.	7.30	to	8.0 Physical Drill & Rifle Inspection.	PARADE GROUND.
	9.0	to	12.0 Company Drill & Bayonet Fighting.	do.

Capt.
O.C. 2/4th Field Coy.R.E.
60th (London) Division.

2/4TH FIELD COMPANY, R.E.

Programme of Training.

(C)

Sappers.

Programme of Training for week ending April 22nd, 1916.

Ref. O.S. 12E, 1" = 1 mile.

Monday.	7.0. to 7.45. Physical Drill & Rifle inspection.	PARADE GROUND.
	9.30 ~~9.0.~~ to 12.30. Task digging & wire entanglements.	SUTTON VENY FIELD WORKS.
	do: Infantry Instruction party.	DO:
	8.0.p.m. Night entrenchments.	DO:
Tuesday.	7.0. to 7.45. Bayonet Fighting.	PARADE GROUND.
	9.30 ~~9.0.~~ to 12.30. Cordage & use of spars.	CAMP FIELD.
	do: Infantry Instruction party.	SUTTON VENY FIELD WORKS.
	8.0.p.m. Night Entrenchments.	DO:
Wednesday. Regtl. Duty.	7.0. to 7.45. Physical drill & rifle inspection.	PARADE GROUND
	9.30 ~~9.0.~~ to 12.30. Task digging.	SUTTON VENY FIELD WORKS.
	do: Infantry Instruction party.	DO:
	8.0.p.m. Night Entanglements	DO:
Thursday.	7.0. to 7.45. Physical drill & rifle inspection.	PARADE GROUND
	9.0. to 12.30. Route March	SUTTON VENY, CORTON, UPTON LOVELL, HEYTESBURY, SUTTON VENY.
	9.30 ~~9.0.~~ to 12.30. Infantry Instruction party.	SUTTON VENY FIELD WORKS.
	8.0.p.m. Night Entanglements.	DO:
Good Friday.	Church Parade.	
Saturday.	7.0. to 8.0. Physical drill & rifle inspection.	PARADE GROUND.
	9.0. to 12.0. Rifle exercises and Company drill.	DO:

OFFICERS RIDING AND DRIVING CLASSES 2.0.P.M. TO 4.0.P.M. EACH AFTERNOON.

Capt.
O.C.2/4th Field Coy R.E.

2/4TH FIELD COMPANY. R.E.
Programme of Training.
Sappers.

(D)

Programme of Training for week ending April 29th, 1916.

Monday.	7.a.m. to 7.45.a.m.	Physical drill.	PARADE GROUND.
	9.a.m. to 4.30.p.m.	Fieldworks.	FIELDWORKS.
	9.a.m. to 4.30.p.m.	Infantry Instruction party.	DO:
Tuesday.	Regimental duties.		R.E.CAMP.
	9.a.m. to 4.30.p.m.	Infantry Instruction party.	FIELDWORKS.
Wednesday.	7.a.m. to 7.45.a.m.	Bayonet fighting.	PARADE GROUND.
	9.a.m. to 4.30.p.m.	Entanglements.	FIELDWORKS.
	9.a.m. to 4.30.p.m.	Infantry Instruction party.	DO:
Thursday.	7.a.m. to 7.45.a.m.	Rifle exercises.	PARADE GROUND
	9.a.m. to 10.30.a.m.	Cordage and use of spars.	R.E.CAMP
	11.a.m. to 4.30.p.m.	Route March	SUTTON VENY, TYTHERINGTON, HEYTESBURY, BISHOPSTROW, BOREHAM, HENFORDS MARSH, PORE HILL, COCKERTON GREEN, SUTTON VENY.
Friday.	Regimental duties.		R.E.CAMP.
	9.a.m. to 4.30.p.m.	Infantry Instruction party.	FIELDWORKS.
Saturday.	7.a.m. to 7.45.a.m.	Physical drill.	PARADE GROUND.
	9.a.m. to 12.noon	Company and extended order drill.	DO:

Capt.
O.C. 2/4th Field Co: R.E.

UNIT: 2/4th Field Coy. R.E.

Army Form C. 2118.

WAR DIARY for MAY.

INTELLIGENCE SUMMARY.

(Erase heading not required.)

Instructions regarding War Diaries and Intelligence Summaries are contained in F.S. Regs., Part II. and the Staff Manual respectively. Title pages will be prepared in manuscript.

Place	Date	Hour	Summary of Events and Information	Remarks and references to Appendices
SUTTON VENY	May. 1st		Training as per Appendix A.	
	2nd		do.	Divn. Engr. Odrs 104, Pt.2;p.1 2-5-16
			1391 2/Cpl. HUNT, T.W., promoted A/Cpl. & 1535 L/Cpl. NYE, F., to A/g. 2/Cpl.	Divl. Engr. Odrs 109;Pt.2;p.4 8-5-16
			2nd LIEUT. W.B. PERKINS granted further leave from 2nd to 11th May.	
	3rd		Training as per Appendix A.	
	4th		do.	
	5th		do.	
			1 Sergt. & 46 other ranks returned from Pontooning Course at CHRISTCHURCH.	
			1438 DRIVER ROBERTS, R., 1783 SAPPER STEPHENSON, N., transferred from Hqrs. 60th (Lon) Divsl. Engrs. R.E. to 2/4th Field Coy. R.E.	T.F. Records 2004/R.E.2, 3-5-16.
			1443 DRIVER HOLVEY, E., & 1393 DRIVER EVEREST, transferred from 2/4th Field Coy. R.E. to Hqrs. 60th (Lon.) Divsl. Engrs.	do.
			Discharge of 2257 SAPPER MARKHAM, E., cancelled.	T.F. Records 1436/R.E.2, 2-5-16.
	6th		Training as per Appendix A.	
			2nd LIEUT. P. LANE, returned to duty from Sick Leave.	
			1 Officer & 12 other ranks (rear party) returned from Pontooning Course at CHRISTCHURCH.	

2.

Army Form C. 2118.

WAR DIARY
or
INTELLIGENCE SUMMARY.
(Erase heading not required.)

Instructions regarding War Diaries and Intelligence Summaries are contained in F.S. Regs., Part II. and the Staff Manual respectively. Title pages will be prepared in manuscript.

Place	Date	Hour	Summary of Events and Information	Remarks and references to Appendices
SUTTON VENY.	May. 8th		Training as per Appendix B.	
	9th		do.	
	10th		do.	
	11th		do.	
			Capt. C.C. CHESTER, R.E.T., reported for duty.	
	12th		3083 Sapper LAKE, F.E. & 3106 Sapper CARPENTER, H., transferred from 3/4th Lon. Field Coy.R.E.	Divn.Egnr.Ordrs 114,Pt.2,p.4 13-5-16.
			Training as per Appendix B.	
	13th		2nd LIEUT. W.B. PERKINS granted further leave from 12th to 21st May.	
			Training as per Appendix B.	
	15th		Training as per Appendix C.	
			CAPT. G.G. OMMANNEY, attached, left this station.	H.Q.Divn.A/ 2173/2, 13-5-16
			2262 SAPPER McKEE, E., proceeded to ROMSEY to attend Course of Cold Shoeing.	H.Q.Divn.Q/498/ 6, 7-5-16.
			A working party of 1 N.C.O. & 8 men attached to 2/7th Lon. Bde,R.F.A. No. 4 Camp, CORTON.	H.Q.Divn.116/ 163, 17-5-16.
	16th		Training as per Appendix C.	
	17th		do.	
			1667 DRIVER MORTON, A., proceeded to WEELEY, Essex, to join 7th Provl. Field Coy.R.E.	T.F.Records 2127/R.E.2 10-5-16.

T2134. Wt. W708—776. 500000. 4/15. Sw J.C. & S.

Army Form C. 2118.

WAR DIARY
or
INTELLIGENCE SUMMARY.
(Erase heading not required.)

Instructions regarding War Diaries and Intelligence Summaries are contained in F. S. Regs., Part II. and the Staff Manual respectively. Title pages will be prepared in manuscript.

Place	Date	Hour	Summary of Events and Information	Remarks and references to Appendices
SUTTON VENY.	May.			
	18th		Ceremonial Drill.	
	19th		Training as per Appendix C.	
	20th		Coy. inspected by C.R.E.	
	22nd		Training as per Appendix D.	
	23rd		1 N.C.O. & 8 men returned from 2/7th Bde. R.F.A., CORTON. Field works & spar bridging.	
	24th		Divisional Route March.	
	25th		Training as per Appendix D. Transfer of 2nd LIEUT. W.B. PERKINS to 3rd Line Depot.	W.O. letter 9/Engineers/ 5350.T.F.3. (M.B.) 21-5-16
	26th		Divisional Trench Attack.	
	27th		Training as per Appendix D.	
	28th		LIEUT. S.G. KILLINGBACK returned from Course of Instruction in Mounted Duties, ALDERSHOT.	
	29th		Preparing ground for Review by H.M. the KING at NORTH FARM.	
	30th		Divisional Review rehearsal at NORTH·FARM. 1751 PTE. HOGG, F.G., R.A.M.C., reported for Water Duties.	

T2134. Wt. W708-776. 500000. 4/15. Sir J. C. & S.

Army Form C. 2118.

WAR DIARY
or
INTELLIGENCE SUMMARY.
(Erase heading not required.)

Instructions regarding War Diaries and Intelligence Summaries are contained in F.S. Regs., Part II and the Staff Manual respectively. Title pages will be prepared in manuscript.

Place	Date	Hour	Summary of Events and Information	Remarks and references to Appendices
SUTTON VENY.	31st		Review by H.M. the KING.	

Capt.
O.C. 2/4th Field Coy. R.E.
60th (London) Division.

2/4th Field Company R.E.

Programme of Training.

Sappers.

Programme of training for week ending May 6th 1916.

Monday.   REGIMENTAL DUTIES.
    6-30 a.m.   Check Parade &   PARADE GROUND.
                                              Rifle Inspection.
    9-0 a.m. to 1-30 p.m.   Infantry Instruction
                                              Party.   FIELD WORKS.

    3-0 p.m. to 4-0 p.m.   Bayonet Fighting.   PARADE GROUND.

Tuesday.
    7-0 a.m. to 7-45 a.m.   Running & Physical   "   "
                                              Drill.
    9-0 a.m. to 1-30 p.m.   Infantry Instruction
                                              Party.   FIELD WORKS.
    3-0 p.m. to 6-0 p.m.   Knotting & Lashing,
                                              Spar Bridging.   PARADE GROUND.

Wednesday.
    7-0 a.m. to 7-45 a.m.   Bayonet Fighting.   "   "

    9-0 a.m. to 12-30 p.m.   Route March.   SUTTON VENY, TYTHER-
                                                                         INGTON, HEYTESBURY,
                                                                         BISHOPSTROW, BOREHAM,
                                                                         HENSFORDS MARSH, PORE
                                                                         -HILL, COCKERTON GREEN
                                                                         SUTTON VENY.
                                                                         O.S. ½" to 1 MILE.

    8-0 p.m. to 11-0 p.m.   Infantry Instruction
                                              Party.   FIELD WORKS.

Thursday.   REGIMENTAL DUTIES.
    6-30 a.m.   Rifle Inspection.   PARADE GROUND.
    9-0 a.m. to 4-30 p.m.   Pontooning.   LONGLEAT PARK.

Friday.
    7-0 a.m. to 7-45 a.m.   Bomb Throwing
                                              Instruction.   VEHICLE PARK.
    9-0 a.m. to 12-30 p.m.   Field Works.   FIELD WORKS.

    8-0 p.m. to 11-0 p.m.   Infantry Instruction
                                              Party.   "   "

Saturday.
    7-0 a.m. to 7-45 a.m.   Physical Drill.   PARADE GROUND.

    9-0 a.m. to 12-0 noon.   Company and Extended
                                              order drill.   "   "

Captain. R.E.T.
O.C. 2/4th Field Company

"B"

2/4th FIELD COMPANY, R.E.T.

Programme of Training.

DISMOUNTED.

Programme of Training for week ending May 13th, 1916.

Ref. O.S. 122, 1" = 1 mile.

Monday.	7.0 to 7.45	Bomb throwing exercises.	WAGON PARK.
	9.0 to 12.30	Brushwood, hurdles, gabions and fascines.	do.
	2.0 to 4.30	Demolitions.	do.
Tuesday.	7.0 to 7.45	Bayonet fighting.	PARADE GROUND.
	9.0 to 4.30	Pontooning.	LONGLEAT PARK.
Wednesday.	REGIMENTAL DUTIES.		
	7.0 to 7.45	Bayonet fighting.	PARADE GROUND.
	9.0 to 4.30	Knotting and lashing.	do.
Thursday.	7.0 to 7.45	Physical drill.	do.
	9.0 to 4.30	Spar bridging.	WAGON PARK.
Friday.	7.0 to 7.45	Bayonet fighting.	PARADE GROUND.
	9.0 to 12.30	Wire entanglements & Demolitions.	FIELD WORKS.
	8.0 p.m. to 10.30 p.m.	Field works.	do.
Saturday.	REGIMENTAL DUTIES.		
	7.0 to 7.45	Bomb throwing exercises.	PARADE GROUND.
	9.0 to 12.0	Company & Extended order drill and Bayonet fighting.	do.

Capt.
O.C. 2/4th Field Coy. R.E.
60th (London) Division.

2/4th FIELD COMPANY, R.E.

Programme of Training.

DISMOUNTED.

Programme of Training for week ending May 20th, 1916.

Ref.O.S. 122, 1" - 1 mile.

Monday.	7.0	to	7.45 Bayonet fighting.	PARADE GROUND.
	9.0	to	4.30 Field works.	FIELD WORKS.
Tuesday.	7.0	to	7.45 Physical drill.	PARADE GROUND.
	9.0	to	4.30 Spar bridging.	HENSFORD MARSH.
Wednesday.	7.0	to	7.45 Bayonet fighting.	PARADE GROUND.
	9.0	to	4.30 Pontooning.	LONGLEAT PARK.
Thursday.	7.0	to	7.45 Rifle exercises.	PARADE GROUND.
	9.0	to	4.30 Route march.	SUTTON VENY, LONGBRIDGE DEVERILL, SHEAR WATER, SHEAR CROSS, CROCKERTON GREEN, SUTTON VENY. Ref.O.S. 122, 1" - 1 mile.
Friday.	7.0	to	7.45 Bomb throwing exercises	PARADE GROUND.
	9.0	to	12.30 Demolitions & Entanglements.	FIELD WORKS.
	8.30	to	11p.m. Obstacles & extention of working parties.	do.
Saturday.	7.0	to	7.45 Physical drill.	PARADE GROUND.
	9.0	to	12.0 Company & extended order drill.	do.

Capt.
O.C. 2/4th Field Coy. R.E.
60th (London) Division.

2/4th FIELD COMPANY, R.E.

Programme of Training.

DISMOUNTED.

Programme of Training for week ending May 27th, 1916.

Monday.	REGIMENTAL DUTIES.			
	7.0 to 7.45	Bayonet fighting.		PARADE GROUND.
	9.0 to 12.30	Wire entanglements.		CAMP.
	2.0 to 4.30	Straw ropes & Mats.		"
Tuesday.	7.0 to 7.45	Rifle exercises.		PARADE GROUND.
	9.0 to 12.30	Spar bridging.		CAMP.
	2.0 to 4.30	Obstacles & automatic alarms.		FIELD WORKS.
Wednesday.		Divisional Route March.		
Thursday. REGTL. DUTIES.	7.0 to 7.45	Physical & Bombing drill.		PARADE GROUND.
	9.0 to 12.30	Wire entanglements.		CAMP.
	2.0 to 4.30	Splicing.		"
Friday.		Divisional Trench Attack.		
Saturday.	7.0 to 7.45	Bayonet fighting.		PARADE GROUND.
	9.0 to 12.0	Company & Extended order Drill.		"

Capt.
O.C. 2/4th Field Coy.R.E.
60th (London) Division.

Army Form C. 2118.

WAR DIARY
or
INTELLIGENCE-SUMMARY.
(Erase heading not required.)

Instructions regarding War Diaries and Intelligence Summaries are contained in F. S. Regs., Part II. and the Staff Manual respectively. Title pages will be prepared in manuscript.

Place	Date	Hour	Summary of Events and Information	Remarks and references to Appendices
Sutton Veny	1.6.		Training as per Appendix A.	
"	2.6.		do: do:	
"	3.6.		Foot Inspection. Training as per Appendix A.	
"	4.6.		Church Parade.	
"	5.6.		Training as per Appendix B. Draft from 3/4th Field Coy Esher. 9 men.	
"	6.6.		do: do:	
"	7.6.		do: do: Transfer of 2624.Sapper Hare.F. to Divsl R.E.Hdqrs vice L/Cp.Leggs.D.	
"	8.6.		Foot-Inspection. Training as per Appendix B. Transfer of 3148.Spr.Troubridgen.3152.Spr.Mansfield to 7th Prov. Field Co:	
"	9.6.		Training as per Appendix B.	
"	10.6.		Foot inspection. Training as per Appendix B.	
"	11.6.		Church Parade.	
"	12.6.		Training as per Appendix C	
"	13.6.		do: do:	
"	14.6.		do: do:	
"	15.6.		do: do:	
"	16.6.		do: do:	
"	17.6.		do: do: Foot inspection.	

Army Form C. 2118.

WAR DIARY
or
INTELLIGENCE-SUMMARY

(Erase heading not required.)

Instructions regarding War Diaries and Intelligence Summaries are contained in F.S. Regs., Part II. and the Staff Manual respectively. Title Pages will be prepared in manuscript.

Place	Date	Hour	Summary of Events and Information	Remarks and references to Appendices
Sutton Veny.	18.6		Transfer to 3/2nd London Divsl. R.E. Esher, 2nd Lt.H.V.Shove. Authority W.D.65844 of 17/3 Inst. " " 3/2nd Home Counties Field Co: Capt.O.C.Chester. S.C.Telegram A27/A1 of 17/3 Inst " " 3/3rd London Field.Co: R.E. 2nd. Lieut. A.C. Brown. Remuster: 5165. Sapper Sinfield.W.C. to Driver. 1878. Sapper Godwin.G. qualified as a Cold Shoer, in accordance with War Office letter 43/Misc/1319, dated August 4th, 1915.	
"	19.6		Training as per Appendix D.	
	20.6		do: do: ~~Inspection by C.R.E. ready for~~	
	21.6		Inspection by C.R.E.ready for move Overseas.	
	22.6		Move of Company Overseas.	

Capt.
O.C.3/4th Field Co: R.E.
60th(London)Division.
21st June, 1916.

2449 Wt. W14957/M90 750,000 1/16 J.B.C. & A. Forms/C.2118/12.

2/4th FIELD COMPANY, R.E. *Appendix A*

Dismounted Section.

PROGRAMME OF TRAINING.

Programme of Training for week ending June 3rd, 1916.

Ref. O.S. 122, 1 inch - 1 mile

Monday.	7.0 to 7.45	Bomb throwing exercises.	PARADE GROUND.
	9.0 to 12.0	Company Drill (Drivers to attend)	do.
	2.0 to 4.0	Bayonet fighting & Gas helmet instruction.	do.
Tuesday.	7.0 to 7.45	Physical drill & Gas helmet instruction.	do.
	9.0 to 10.0	Company drill (Drivers to attend)	do.
	10.0 to 12.0	C.R.E.'s parade (dismounted)	do.
	2.0 to 4.0	Bombing & wire entanglements	CAMP
Wednesday.		REGIMENTAL DUTIES. Inspection.	
Thursday.	7.0 to 7.45	~~Bombing exercises & Gas helmet instruction.~~ Physical drill.	PARADE GROUND.
	9.0 to 4.30	Pontooning.	LONGLEAT PARK.
Friday.	7.0 to 7.45	Bombing exercises & Gas helmet instruction.	PARADE GROUND.
	9.0 to 4.30	Route March.	SUTTON VENY, LONG-BRIDGE DEVERILL, X roads 500 X N of LOWER BARN FARM, SHUTE FARM, SHEAR WATER, SHEAR CROSS, CROCKERTON GREEN, SOUTHLEIGH WOOD, SUTTON VENY.
Saturday.		REGIMENTAL DUTIES.	
	7.0 to 7.45	Bomb throwing exercises.	PARADE GROUND.
	9.0 to 12.0	Company & Extended order drill & Rifle exercises.	do.

Capt.
O.C. 2/4th Field Coy. R.E.
60th (London) Division.

Appendix B

COMPANY R.E.

Programme of Training.

DISMOUNTED SECTION.

Programme of Training for week ending June 10th, 1916.

Ref O.S.12W. 1" = 1 mile.

Monday.	7.0. to 7.45.	Rifle exercises	PARADE GROUND.
	9.0. to 12.0.	Field Works & Demolitions	FIELD WORKS.
	2.0. to 4.0.	Bombing, bayonet fighting, & gas helmet instruction.	
Tuesday. REGTL. DUTIES.	7.0. to 7.45.	Bayonet fighting and gas helmet instruction.	PARADE GROUND
	9.0. to 4.0.	Cordage and use of spars, spar bridging.	CAMP
Wednesday.	7.0. to 7.45.	Bomb throwing and gas helmet instruction.	PARADE GROUND.
	9.0. to 4.0.	Pontooning	LONGLEAT PARK.
Thursday.	7.0. to 7.45.	Bayonet fighting.	PARADE GROUND
	9.0. to 12.0.	Field Works.	FIELD WORKS.
	2.0. to 4.0.	Knotting and Splicing, Wire entanglements.	CAMP.
Friday. REGTL DUTIES.	7.0. to 7.45.	Physical drill	PARADE GROUND
	9.0. to 4.0.	Route March	SUTTON VENY, CROCKERTON GREEN, WARMINSTER, BISHOPSTROW, NORTON BAVANT, SUTTON VENY.
Saturday.	7.0. to 7.45.	Physical drill, bombing exercise.	PARADE GROUND.
	9.0. to 12.0.	Company and extended order drill. Gas helmet instruction.	DO:

Capt.
O.C.2/4th Field Co: R.E.
60th (London) Division.

2/4 London 2/d Coy

Vol 1

WAR DIARY
or
INTELLIGENCE SUMMARY

Army Form C. 2118

(Erase heading not required.)

Instructions regarding War Diaries and Intelligence Summaries are contained in F.S. Regs., Part II. and the Staff Manual respectively. Title Pages will be prepared in manuscript.

Place	Date	Hour	Summary of Events and Information	Remarks and references to Appendices
SUTTON VENY	22/6	2.am	First half of Coy. left for WARMINSTER STATION and entrained at 4.50 am.	
			Arrived SOUTHAMPTON DOCKS 7 am	
		3.am	Second half of Coy. left for WARMINSTER STATION and entrained at 5.50 am	
SOUTHAMPTON		6 pm	Company embarked in two parties 5 Officers 154 other ranks on "INVENTOR"	
			2 Officers 54 other ranks on CONNAUGHT	
HAVRE	23/6	7.30am	100f disembarked	
		11.15am	Proceeded to DOCKS REST CAMP	
DO	24/6	9.am	Left REST CAMP for GOODS STATION and entrained. Train departed at 12.30 pm	
ST. POL	25/6	5 am	Coy. detrained and marched to PENIN. Billeted at DOFFINES FARM	
PENIN	26/6	6.pm	Coy. left DOFFINES FARM and marched to MAROEUIL arriving at 11.pm.	
MAROEUIL	28/6		Sections 1,2,3,14 attached to 1/1st HIGHLAND FIELD COY. R.E. for instruction	
DO	30/6	11.am	MAJOR D.F. COLSON arrived	
		3.pm	M. VIDAL (Interpreter) reported for duty	
			1266 Sapper RALPH. J left to report to Div Trans for duty as loader.	

[signature] Capt
O.C. 2/4th LONDON FIELD COY. R.E.

Appendix D

2/4th Field Co: R.E.

Programme of Training.

DISMOUNTED SECTION.

Programme of work for week ending June 24th, 1916.

Ref. O.S. 122. 1" - 1 mile.

Monday.	7.0. to 7.45.	Physical drill.	PARADE GROUND.
	9.0. to 4.30.	Pontoon bridging.	LONGLEAT PARK.
	9.0. to 4.30.	Dug-outs.	FIELDWORKS.
Tuesday.	7.0. to 7.45.	Gas helmet exercise.	PARADE GROUND.
	9.0. to 4.30.	Fieldworks & dug-outs.	FIELDWORKS.
Wednesday.	7.0. to 7.45.	Bayonet fighting exercises.	PARADE GROUND.
REGTL. DUTIES.	9.0. to 4.30.	Cordage & use of spars & field geometry.	WAGON PARK.
Thursday.	7.0. to 7.45.	Gas helmet exercises.	PARADE GROUND.
	9.0. to 4.30.	Route March.	SUTTON VENY, WARMINSTER, CROCKERTON GREEN, LONGBRIDGE DEVERILL, SUTTON VENY.
Friday.	7.0. to 7.45.	Bayonet fighting instruction.	PARADE GROUND.
	9.0. to 4.30.	Fieldworks.	FIELDWORKS.
Saturday.	7.0. to 7.45.	Rifle exercise.	PARADE GROUND.
REGTL. DUTIES.	9.0. to 12.0.	Squad and Section drill.	PARADE GROUND.

(signature)
Capt.
O.C. 2/4th Field Co: R.E.
60th (London) Division.

Appendix C

2/4th Field Co: R.E.

Programme of training.

DISMOUNTED SECTION.

Programme of work for week ending June 17th, 1916.

Ref. O.S. 122. 1" - 1 mile.

Monday. REGTL. DUTIES.	7.0. to 7.45.	Physical training. Gas helmet instruction.	Parade Ground
	9.0. to 12.0.	Sapping &c.	Field Works
	2.0. to 4.0.	Bombing and Gas helmet instruction.	Camp.
Tuesday.	7.0. to 7.45.	Rifle Exercises. Gas helmet instruction.	Parade Ground.
	9.0. to 12.0.	Wire entanglements and alarms.	Camp.
	2.0. to 4.0.	Bombing (live bombs) and demolitions	Bombing Ground.
Wednesday.	7.0. to 7.45.	Bayonet fighting. Gas helmet instruction.	Parade Ground.
	9.0. to 4.0.	Pontooning.	Longleat Park.
Thursday. REGTL. DUTIES.	7.0. to 7.45.	Bombing and bayonet fighting gas helmet instruction.	Parade Ground.
	9.0. to 4.0.	Cordage and use of spars spar bridging knotting & lashing.	Camp.
Friday.	7.0. to 7.45.	Physical drill. Gas helmet instruction.	Parade Ground.
	9.0. to 4.0.	Route March. (During this Gas Helmets are to be put on).	Sutton Veny, Bishopstrow, Norton Bavant, Heytesbury, Upton Lovell. Corton, Tykerington, Sutton Veny.
Saturday.	7.0. to 7.45.	Physical drill and gas helmet instruction.	Parade Ground.
	9.0. to 12.0.	Company and extended order drill with gas helmets.	do:

Capt.
for O.C.2/4th Field Co: R.E.
60th (London) Division.

COPY

WAR DIARY
or
INTELLIGENCE SUMMARY. 2/4th LONDON FIELD COY

(Erase heading not required.)

Instructions regarding War Diaries and Intelligence Summaries are contained in F. S. Regs., Part II. and the Staff Manual respectively. Title pages will be prepared in manuscript.

Place	Date 1916	Hour	Summary of Events and Information
MAROEUIL	July 1		95% 2/Lt REVELEY J.E.W. 2 Sgts R.O.&E H.E attacked to 6th W. ENG HQS. for duty. 3/168 Sgt HOPPER E. Reprimanded as Serving Smith as from June 23 1916.
LEFT OF DOUAI BRARD STREET	9 10		Sentry post R.O. W3 & W4 July 5 19.7. MG SENTRY POST 80% complete MG EMPLACEMENT Work on sap tank Reg. Ord. 30% complete
UPPR T. PT. PULPIT MAROEUIL	11		SIGNAL POST erected 3/108 Sgt CRUMBLE F.G. 1920 Sapper CARD D. 3153 Sapper WOOD H.C attached to 6th LONDON FIELD COY R.E. attached for duty from B.O.S. DE BRAY for duty & return 2/247 Cpl MOODY H.W. 1m/m 1/6 LONDON FIELD COY R.E. attached for return
ZIVY MERCIER	12		OBSERVATION POST erected SIGNAL POST after ng ~ 95% complete (1st to 12th) TRANSMITTING LOOPHOLE on site 95% complete (1 to 12)
ENTATA REDT MAROEUIL	12 midnight		Coy relieved 1/1st HIGHLAND FIELD COY R.E. SIGNAL OBSERVATION POST complete
AV- DES-AUBIS OCADE AVENUE CLAUDOT			CUPOLA 25% complete (Work advanced) MG EMPLACEMENT complete
LABYRINTH REDT MAROEUIL	13		Trenches 28% complete Trench 359 complete Lumberg entrance to Dug-out 80% complete Down Alt. L. RANK. J. Company attached for duty and return Engr Yus. 3 Summers 1 Sapper R.F.A attached for return
MERCIER MAROEUIL	14 15		TRENCH RAILWAY 150 yards laid (1st to 13th) Sapper M.M.P attached for return 2/Lt P.LANE 1198 Cpl HEAD H.J. 231 Cpl WALKER A.H left to attend course in ANTI GAS measures at FREVIN CAPELLE
	16		1993 Sap JONES H.W. evacuated to 30 Casualty Clearing Station Sapper of Saw Bay and Board ½ day 4351 Sapper — man attached for return
	17 18		2/Lt P.LANE 1198 Cpl HEAD H.J. 231 Cpl WALKER A.H return ref/fr. after attending course in ANTI GAS MEASURES
CLAUDOT	19		Refer to Pan Y complete

Army Form C. 2118.

WAR DIARY
or
INTELLIGENCE SUMMARY.
(Erase heading not required.)

Place	Date	Hour	Summary of Events and Information	Remarks and references to Appendices
MAREUIL EN FORGES ELBE	July 20		2/Lt H. Moody NW returned 15 1/6th LONDON FIELD COY R.E. Enemy aeroplane to complain.	
			Enemy Infantry Kayfly.	
MAREUIL	23		Six Alt Kayfly men 303 Bde RFA attached for rations	
			2 Lt BENNETT 1 INDIAN FIELD SQUADRON attached for rations.	
			Enemy RFA MG Rocket SK	
	24		Actions of enemy Arty Rocket attacks for rations	
			Machine RFA (attached) for rations possible	
	25		LT. SG KILLING BACK 12.10 Cpl GARNER att 11289 Cpl HIDER N left 15 att'd Coy in FREVIN CAPELLE	
			ANTI GAS MEASURES at FREVIN CAPELLE	
VARSE	26		Nil. Preri.	
MAREUIL	27		LT. SG KILLING BACK 12.10 Cpl GARNER att 11289 Cpl HIDER W left to Coy in FREVIN CAPELLE	
			Lt. Starling Comee in ANTI GAS MEASURES	
	29		0 + 0 HQ + 22 OR 2/4th BATT LON REGT attached for rations and instruction in	
			Battery Arrangements.	
TERRITORIAL AV	30		Enemy Aeroplane complete	
MAREUIL			1190 2 Cpl PELLIS FC wounded.	
BESSANT				
LAUDOT JUNC	31		Nat. Supply Work in hand	
FIRING LINE			Returned Amplification trenches 2308 yards completed 209 yards trench Boardwalk	
			109 Burnt pit dug. (13'x3'x3')	
R.E. SHELTERS			Dug out complete. (13'x3'x3')	
NR GLASGOW DUMP			Eng Nos 1 & 2 "PLT-bys" commenced LA TARGETTE & TERRITORIAL PUMP	
BESSANT			Work commenced on trench with entanglement	

(Signed) G.O.S. Gaujau
Capt.
for O.C. 2/4th Lond Field Coy R.E.

Certified true copy.

A5834 Wt.W4973/M687 750,000 8/16 D. D. & L. Ltd. Forms/C.2118/13

2/Lt
O.C. 2/4th Lond Coy R.E.

WAR DIARY.

2/4th LONDON FIELD COY R.E.

AUGUST 1916

Army Form C. 2118

WAR DIARY 2/1st LONDON FIELD COY RE

INTELLIGENCE SUMMARY

(Erase heading not required.)

Instructions regarding War Diaries and Intelligence Summaries are contained in F. S. Regs., Part II. and the Staff Manual respectively. Title Pages will be prepared in manuscript.

Place	Date	Hour	Summary of Events and Information	Remarks and references to Appendices
MARŒUIL	AUGUST 1st		1190 II Cpl PELLS. F.C. evacuated to H.2 casualty Clearing Station. Fine and very warm. Wind S. to S.E.	
	2nd		Alteration to Pipe line at BESSAN TRENCH completed. Cloudy forenoon, Afternoon Clear, night	
	"		1 LT. A.F NEAL. 128th Cpl GOLDSWORTHY R. & 1281 Cpl JONES WE proceeded to FREVIN CAPELLE to attend Anti-Gas Course	
	"		2. T.M Emplacements STONE ST Completed	
	3rd		Fine - dry.	
	4th	1-0 p.m.	2159 Sapper WOODS G.H reported for duty from reinforcement camp Fine, cloudy later.	
	5th		1 LT. A.F NEAL. 128th Cpl GOLDSWORTHY R & 1281 Cpl JONES WE reported on conclusion of Anti-Gas course at FREVIN CAPELLE	
	"		Fine.	
	6th		T M Emplacement STONE ST completed Excavation of Pipe trench W. of BETHUNE ROAD completed Excavation of Tank Emplacement ELBE TRENCH completed 1 officer and 22 other ranks 2/1st LONDON REGT. returned to unit on completion of Course	

WAR DIARY 2/4th LONDON FIELD COY RE

INTELLIGENCE SUMMARY

Army Form C. 2118

AUGUST 1916.

Place	Date	Hour	Summary of Events and Information	Remarks and references to Appendices
MAROEUIL	August 6th		Continued	
	"		Course in hasty wire Entanglements	
	"		2583 Driver COWLING W.B. transferred from 2/4th LONDON FIELD CO. R.E. to 60th DIV RE HD QRS. 1396 Driver HOWARD A.R transferred from 60th DIV RE HQ to 2/4th LONDON FIELD COY R.E	
	7th/8th		2 Lt BENNETT 1st INDIAN FIELD SQDN returned to unit. Overcast in forenoon, clearer later.	
	"		1190 2Cpl PELLS F.C. discharged from H.42 C.C. STN. to Divisional Rest Camp 1848 L/Cpl SCHOLZ L. R.A.M.C. evacuated to H.42 C.C STN Fine cloudy later.	
	9th		1204 SERGT: HARRIS T.E attached to 60th DIV ENG HQ as instructor to brats, Consolidation School	
	"		2" pipe line W. of BETHUNE ROAD completed, left tank installed at BESSAN Tank Emplacement Fine	

WAR DIARY 2/1st LONDON FIELD COY. R.E.

INTELLIGENCE SUMMARY

Army Form C. 2118

(Erase heading not required.)

Instructions regarding War Diaries and Intelligence Summaries are contained in F.S. Regs., Part II. and the Staff Manual respectively. Title Pages will be prepared in manuscript.

Place	Date	Hour	Summary of Events and Information	Remarks and references to Appendices
MAROEUIL	10th		1183 SERGT. EVERITT H.G. "A" Battery 300 Brigade R.F.A. returned to unit. Connections at VASE TANK completed and value boxes installed. Fine. Rain in morning.	
"	11th	A.M 12.30	Killed in action LIEUT S.G. KILLINGBACK 1186 SAPPER SCANES. L.D. 3128 SAPPER JONES W.W. Whilst consolidating a mine crater at Sheet 51B NW Edn 2B A4 3.4. Fine. Heavy mist at night.	
"	12th	3.30pm	829 SAPPER GUENIGAULT E. proceeded to 3rd Army HdQrs for carpentry course. 1186 SAPPER SCANES. L.D. 3128 SAPPER JONES W.W. buried at BRITISH CEMETERY MAROEUIL Sheet 51C NE "B" Series F 27 A 9.4	
"	13th		Heavy mist early morning – blew later. Pile connections at M2 Tanks completed.	
"	14th	12.30pm	LIEUT. S.G. KILLINGBACK buried at BRITISH CEMETERY MAROEUIL Sheet 51C NE "B" Series F 27 A 9.4 Rain early morning. Fine cloudy evening.	
"	15th		Fine, with occasional heavy rain. Wind W. Erection of Tank house at BESSAN JUNC: completed.	

AUGUST 1916

Army Form C. 2118

WAR DIARY 2/1st London Field Co. RE
INTELLIGENCE SUMMARY
(Erase heading not required.)

Instructions regarding War Diaries and Intelligence Summaries are contained in F.S. Regs., Part II. and the Staff Manual respectively. Title Pages will be prepared in manuscript.

Place	Date	Hour	Summary of Events and Information	Remarks and references to Appendices
MAROEUIL	15th		Preliminary survey of VISTULA RAILWAY completed	
	16th		Showery Wind W.S.W.	
	17th		So So	
			13848 L/CPL. SCHOLZ L.A. discharged from No. 2 C.C. Stn. to No.16 Convalescent Camp	
			Survey of VISTULA RAILWAY completed	
			Showery	
	18th		1286 SERGT. HYEM J.D. evacuated to No.19 C.C. Stn.	
			137 II CPL. CHUBB W. reported for duty	
			Tank emplacement at BESSAN LEFT completed	
			Showery	
	19th		100 L.D. horses arrived from Mobile Veterinary Section	
			Showery	
	20th		VASE TANKS Water put through tanks	
	21st		Fine	
	22nd		So	
	23rd		So	
			Tank House completed at BESSAN JUNE (main tank)	

WAR DIARY 2/1st LONDON FIELD COY R.E.

INTELLIGENCE SUMMARY

Army Form C. 2118

AUGUST 1916

Instructions regarding War Diaries and Intelligence Summaries are contained in F.S. Regs., Part II. and the Staff Manual respectively. Title Pages will be prepared in manuscript.

(Erase heading not required.)

Place	Date	Hour	Summary of Events and Information	Remarks and references to Appendices
MAROEUIL	23rd		Pipes repaired at VESE TANK (Completed)	CRYC
	24th		2 LIEUT. A.F. NEAL and H8 O.R. attached to 3/1st LONDON FIELD COY R.E. for duty. Fine Showery afternoon.	RYC
	25th		Cloudy. Wind S.W.	RYC
			One Bay on Completed at PARIS REDOUBT.	
			Tank Emplacement at RHINE SHELTERS Completed	
			Pipe line connection completed at BESSAN RIGHT TANK	
			ARIANE RAILWAY Repairs to Line Completed	
			1210. CPL GARNER A.H. promoted A/SERGT to date from 18th AUG 1916	
	26th		Fine morning. Overcast afternoon. Wind S.W.	RYC
	27th		Forenoon Showery afternoon fine Wind S.W.	RYC
			BESSAN RIGHT TANK Emplacement Completed	
			829 SAPPER GUENIGAULT. E reported on conclusion of Cookery Course at 3rd Army Hd: Qrs:	
	28th		Fine and Cloudy at intervals. Showers. Wind S.W.	
			3101 SAPPER CHESTERMAN W.M. Reported for duty (Reinforcement) from 3/1st LOND.F.R.E.	

WAR DIARY 2/1st LONDON FIELD COY. R.E.
INTELLIGENCE SUMMARY

AUGUST 1916 — Army Form C. 2118

Place	Date	Hour	Summary of Events and Information	Remarks and references to Appendices
MARDEUIL	28th		LIEUT A F WILLIAMS and 2339 Dr se CROGAN EC (BATMAN) reported to OC Special Works Park WIMEREUX for course of instruction on camouflage commencing 29th August 1916.	
	29th		One L.D. horse destroyed for veterinary reasons. Afternoon showery, afternoon fine. Wind W. Tank emplacement at BESSAN RAILHEAD completed. Tank at CLAUDOT WELL installed. Stormy. Heavy rain. Wind W.	
	30th		Stormy. Wind S.S.W.	
	31st		One L.D. horse received from Mobile Veterinary Section. Repairs to "FIRING LINE" 1st to 31st AUG 1294 Yards TRENCH deepened 1294 Yards Trench boards laid 91 Sump pits dug Repairs to DOUAI Trench 26th to 29th AUG. 169 Yards Trench drained, 169 Yards boards laid Repairs to VASE 115 Yards Trench drained 16 Yards boards laid	

AUGUST 1916

WAR DIARY 2/1st LONDON FIELD COY R.E.

or

INTELLIGENCE SUMMARY

Army Form C. 2118

(Erase heading not required.)

Place	Date	Hour	Summary of Events and Information	Remarks and references to Appendices
MAROEUIL	31st		Heather Lane	

[signature]
CAPTAIN R.E.T.
for OC 2/1st LONDON FIELD COY. R.E.

Vol 4

WAR DIARY

2/4TH LONDON FIELD COY. R.E.

SEPTEMBER 1916.

SEPTEMBER 1916

WAR DIARY — 2/4TH LONDON FIELD COY. R.E.

INTELLIGENCE SUMMARY

Army Form C. 2118

Place	Date	Hour	Summary of Events and Information	Remarks and references to Appendices
MARCEUIL	AUG 31st		2625 SAPPER EDGELL P.W. evacuated to 30th Casualty Clearing Station. Weather overcast Wind S.W.	
"	SEPT 1st		Work platform at CLAUDOT WELL completed	
"	"	9.30 am	3143 SAPPER GOLDNEY J.T. proceeded to HAVRE to report to do Base Depot for transfer to Home Service under authority D.A.G. & H.Q. 3rd Echelon C.R. No 55TH/8455/4 Adjt & QMG. Weather fine, overcast at intervals Wind S.W.	
"	"	11 P.M	2nd LT. A F NEAL and M.B. O.R. reported on conclusion of duty with 3/5 L.F. to R.E.	
SEPT 2nd			Weather fine, overcast at intervals Wind S.W.	
"	"	5 P.M	LT. A.F. WILLIAMS and 2334 DRIVER GROGAN E.E. (Batman) reported on conclusion of course in Camouflage at Special Works Park WIMEREUX. 1246 LEE CPL. KERLEY. A and 1848 LEE CPL. SCHOLZ. L.A (R.A.M.C) evacuated to 30th Casualty Clearing Station.	
Sept 3rd			Weather fine wind S.W. to W.	
"	"	4 P.M	1204 SERGT HARRIS T.F. reported on conclusion of duty at School of Bridge Construction at AGNIERES. 639 SERGT JULIEN W.E. proceeded to AGNIERES (in charge) at School of Bridge Construction at AGNIERES. 1182 SAPPER TROLLEY N.G. wounded (slightly)	
SEPT 4th			Weather showery Forenoon fine afternoon Wind S.W. to W. 137 2nd CPL CHUBB'N proceeded to NINE ELMS (N of POPPERINGHE) to report to OC 1/2nd LONDON FIELD COY R.E. for transfer under authority of H.Q. D.A.D. 3rd Echelon C.R. 3349/C dated 24/8/16 2625 SAPPER EDGELL P.W. evacuated from 30th Casualty Clearing Station to Divisional Convalescent Company	

SEPTEMBER 1916

WAR DIARY or **INTELLIGENCE SUMMARY**

2/4th LONDON FIELD Coy R.E. Army Form C. 2118

Instructions regarding War Diaries and Intelligence Summaries are contained in F.S. Regs., Part II. and the Staff Manual respectively. Title Pages will be prepared in manuscript.

(Erase heading not required.)

Place	Date	Hour	Summary of Events and Information	Remarks and references to Appendices
MARŒUIL	SEPT 5th		Weather overcast with rain at intervals	
		10 AM	Sapper HARDCASTLE D.N. R.A.M.C. attached for rations from 60 2 DIV ENGRS HD QTRS also 1 Horse (Rider)	
	SEPT 6th		Weather overcast Foreman J. & Wigmore J. Hmd N.N.W	
		1 PM	Eleven O.R. also 1 Horse and 15 mules attached for duty and rations from 8/9/16	
			1/4th LONDON FIELD Coy.R.E. rationed from 8/9/16	
	SEPT 7th		Weather fine Hmd N.N.E.	
	SEPT 8th		Weather fine Hmd N.E.	
	SEPT 9th		Weather fine Hmd N.N.E.	
		1 PM	102th SAPPER SKINNER P.E. proceeded to 3rd ARMY HD QTRS for course of instruction in copying.	
	SEPT 10th		Weather dull fine at intervals Hmd N.E. to N.	
			Dugouts at BRIGADE HEADQUARTERS completed	
			124416 LCE CPL KERLEY A evacuated from 30th Casualty Clearing Station to Divisional Convalescent Camp	
	SEPT 11th		Weather overcast Hmd N.E. to N.W.	
			8 officers and 57 O.R. detailed to 1/6th LONDON FIELD Coy R.E. for duty and rations from SEPT 14th 1916	
			60 R. 12 Horses and 3 G.S. Wagons returned for duty under 2/Lt TURNER from DIV: AMN: COL: rationed from Sept 13th	
			LT H.M. SOLOMON (of Light Railway) and 2/H16 PTE. STEMP. A.A (Batmen) atth: to Madame	
	SEPT 12		Weather overcast Somt Shower. Hmd S.W.	
			Dug-out at LEFT Coy HD QTRS Completed, Repairs to TRUMAN ST: Trench Completed	

WAR DIARY
INTELLIGENCE SUMMARY

Army Form C. 2118

Place	Date	Hour	Summary of Events and Information	Remarks and references to Appendices
MARŒUIL	Sept 13th		Weather overcast Wind W. Pipe line at VISTULA completed	
			31369 SAPPER PUGSLEY. J. Evacuated to 30th Casualty Clearing Station	
"	Sept 14th		Weather fine cloudy at intervals Wind N.W.	
"	Sept 15th		Weather fine Wind N.W.	
			Returns to TERRITORIAL-MERCIER Branch completed	
"	Sept 16th		Weather fine Wind N.W.	
			2362 DRIVER KING P.G. Evacuated to No 2 Casualty Clearing Station	
"	Sept 17th		Weather fine Wind N.W.	
"	Sept 18th		Weather dull wet Wind S.W.	
			2624 LEE.CPL: HARE.F transferred from 60th DIV ENG. HD QTRS to 2/4th LONDON FIELD COY. R.E. and cease to act as Re-bjt	
			954 LEE CPL. REVELEY. J.F.W. transferred from 2/4th LONDON FIELD COY: R.E. to 60th DIV ENG HD QTRS. Authority T.F. Record Letter No 3941 R.E. 2 dated 11/9/16	
			2nd LT: DAWSON and 2029 GNR: COLE. A. 302 Bde R.F.A. 2621 SERGT CHALKE J.E.	
			403 BOMBR: PERKINS.C. D.A.C. attached for rations	
"	Sept 19th		Weather fine Wind N.W.	
			1443 DRIVER HOLVEY.E. transferred from H.Q. 60th DIV. ENGRS to 2/4th LONDON FIELD COY.R.E. Authority T.F. Record letter 3941 R.E. 2 d. 11/9/16	
			1815 DRIVER. WRIGHT. W. transferred from 2/4th LONDON FIELD COY R.E. to H.Q. 60th DIV R.E.	
	Sept 19th	1. P.M.	The following Adjusted to reinforcements 13 to 2/4th LONDON FIELD COY R.E.	
			3046 S T.S.S. STEVENS G., 3147 SAP BUTLER.E. 3130 SAP LOVE. F.W. 3353. SAP SQUIRE F.E. from 2/6th L.F.Co R.E. from 3/4th L.F.Co R.E. from 3/2nd L.F.Co R.E. from 3/4th L.F.Co R.E.	
			2608 SAPPER MATTHEWS. H. from 3/4th L.F.Co R.E.	

WAR DIARY

2/1st LONDON FIELD COY R.E Army Form C. 2118

INTELLIGENCE SUMMARY

SEPTEMBER 1916

Place	Date	Hour	Summary of Events and Information	Remarks and references to Appendices
MAROEUIL	SEPT 20		Weather overcast hot. Wind N.W.	
			2 Officers & 54 O.R. detached to 1/1st LONDON FIELD COY R.E. for duty and rations taken on Ration Strength of this unit. VISTULA TANK Emplacement completed.	
"	SEPT 21st		Weather overcast Showery. Wind N.E. 2631 SAPPER BONE J.W. evacuated to 1/42nd Casualty Clearing Station 193 BOMBR PERKINS C. returned to unit. Reverting of approach to BESSAN LEFT TANK HOUSE completed.	
"	SEPT 22nd		Weather fine. Wind S.S.E 1848 LCE CORPL SCHOLZ L.F.(RAMC) evacuated from 30th Casualty Clearing Stn to Reinforcement Camp.	
"	SEPT 23rd		Weather fine. Wind S.E. 6.35PM 1424 SAPPER SKINNER reported on completion of Wiring Course at Third Army H.Q. Quarters 1246 LCE.CPL. KERLEY H. evacuated to 30th Casualty Clearing Stn	
"	SEPT 24th		Weather fine. Wind S.E.	
"	SEPT 25th		Weather fine Wind S.E. LT H.M. SOLOMAN and 2446 PTE STEMP A.H. returned to unit 1382 SAPPER TROLLET W.G. evacuated to 30th Casualty Clearing Stn 2637 " BONE J.W. to reinforcement camp.	
"	SEPT 26th		Weather fine. Wind S.S.E 2nd LT.C.H. TURNER and 1854 DVR COX.A. and 2 horses riders detached to 60th DN ENG H.Q.	

SEPTEMBER 1918

WAR DIARY 2/4th LONDON FIELD COY R.E. Army Form C. 2118

INTELLIGENCE SUMMARY

Instructions regarding War Diaries and Intelligence Summaries are contained in F.S. Regs., Part II. and the Staff Manual respectively. Title Pages will be prepared in manuscript.

(Erase heading not required.)

Place	Date	Hour	Summary of Events and Information	Remarks and references to Appendices
MARCEUIL	SEPT 27th		Weather overcast. Wind S.S.W. 1882 SAPPER TROLLET W.G. evacuated from 30th Casualty Clearing Station to Reinforcement Camp. C.R.A. inspected experimental R.E. Bridge for 13.PDR Q.F Gun.	
"	SEPT 28th		Weather fine. Wind S.E. C.R.E. inspected horse lines etc. 2/Lt C.H.TURNER and 185th DVR.COX. H. & 2 Horses (Riding) returned from 60th DIV ENG'l H.Q.	
"	SEPT 29th		Meeting of Approach Trenches to VISTULA TANKS completed. Weather dull. Wind N.E.	
"	SEPT 30th	1 PM	1198 CORPL. MEAD H.J. proceeded to ROUEN for duty at BASE TRAINING CAMP. Weather fine. Wind N.E. G.O.C. 60th DIVISION inspected billets and horse lines &c.	

FOR O.C. 2/4th LONDON FIELD COY R.E.
CAPTAIN

Confidential

WAR DIARY

2/4th LONDON FIELD COY. R.E.

OCTOBER 1916

OCTOBER 1916 — Army Form C. 2118

WAR DIARY 2/4TH LONDON FIELD COY R.E.
INTELLIGENCE SUMMARY
(Erase heading not required.)

Place	Date	Hour	Summary of Events and Information	Remarks and references to Appendices
MAREUIL	Oct 1st		Weather, morning fine, overcast later. Wind S.E.	W.F.C
			13144 SERGT OUTRED. A.M. proceeded to AGNIERS for duty at Brats Consolidation School	
			529 SERGT JULIEN W.E. reported on conclusion of duty at Brats Consolidation School	
			II LIEUT. N.B. DATE reported for duty	
			1 Draught horse died	
	2nd		Weather wet. Wind S.N. to S.E.	W.F.C
			MAJOR D.F. COLSON proceeded to HERMAVILLE for duty as acting C.R.E.	
			1816 DRIVER BROWN W.J. (BATMAN) also	
			H.O.R 2/14th BATT. L.R reported for duty and rations	
			H.O.R 2/15th " " " "	
			H.O.R 2/16th " " " "	
			Bridge construction in SUPPORT LINE completed	
	3rd		Weather wet, fine later. Wind S.S.W.	W.F.C
			II LIEUT. N.B DATE proceeded to AGNIERS for course of instruction at Brats Consolidation School.	

WAR DIARY

of 2/4th LONDON FIELD COY RE

INTELLIGENCE SUMMARY

(Erase heading not required.)

Army Form C. 2118

OCTOBER 1916

Place	Date	Hour	Summary of Events and Information	Remarks and references to Appendices
MARŒUIL	3rd		5 OR & draught horses 1 Ryder & 2 G.S. Wagons reported for duty and rations from 60th D.A.C.	W.F.C.
			Trench repairs NR BESSAN RAILHEAD completed	
			Three O.R. 2/15th BATT LON REGT returned to unit	
	4th		Weather overcast with rain at intervals. Wmd S.H.	W.F.C.
			Bookhouse at BRIGADE H.Q. completed	
	5th		30116 Spr S. STEVENS G. Demisshed as a Sapper from 1916 BLACKSMITH Skilled. Wmd W	W.F.C.
			Weather fine	
	6th		Weather overcast Wmd S.H.	W.F.C.
	7th		Weather fine Dull. Home rain later. Wmd W	W.F.C.
			Bridge Construction at MINATOUR completed	
	8th		Weather wet Wmd W	W.F.C.
	9th		Weather overcast Wmd W	W.F.C.
	10th		Weather fine Wmd S.H.	W.F.C.
	11th		Weather Dull & Showery Wmd W to S.W.	W.F.C.

WAR DIARY or INTELLIGENCE SUMMARY

2/4th LONDON FIELD COY. R.E.

Army Form C. 2118

OCTOBER 1916

Place	Date	Hour	Summary of Events and Information	Remarks and references to Appendices
MARCEUIL	11th		Pipe line at ADVANCED DRESSING STATION Completed. 3168 DRIVER POTTS T.G. Reported as reinforcement from 2/5th LONDON FIELD COY R.E. 1 O.R 2/18th BATT. LON REGT attacked for rations. 2 O.R and 4 horses (3H.D, 1R, 6M.R) attached for rations from 60th D.A.C also 8 O.S.N. 2263 SAPPER MATTHEWS W. evacuated to 30 Casualty Clearing Station. Weather overcast. Wind N to S.W.	W.F.C
	12th		1 O.R 2/18th BATT L.R. and 1 O.R 2/24th attd. for rations. Construction of bridge trestles at YASE Completed. Weather overcast. Wind W.	W.F.C
	13th		3459 SAPPER PUGSLEY evacuated from 30 C.C.S reported for duty. MAJOR D.F COLSON and 1816 DRIVER BROWN W.T. (batman) reported on conclusion of duty. As Acting C.R.E. 1 Horse (Rider) shot for Veterinary reasons. Weather overcast. Wind W.	W.F.C
	14th		2 LIEUT F.E. PLUMB and 2 LIEUT J.E CHARNLEY returned for duty. 4 O.R 8 Draught Horses & 2 G.S Wagons attached for rations from 60th DAC.	W.F.C

WAR DIARY 2/4TH LONDON FIELD COY R.E.

or

INTELLIGENCE SUMMARY

(Erase heading not required.)

Army Form C. 2118

OCTOBER 1916

Instructions regarding War Diaries and Intelligence Summaries are contained in F.S. Regs., Part II. and the Staff Manual respectively. Title Pages will be prepared in manuscript.

Place	Date	Hour	Summary of Events and Information	Remarks and references to Appendices
MAROEUIL	14th		31b+ Sapper HARRIS C.H. reported for duty from B/ Div TRAIN Weather overcast. Wind N.W.	J.T.C
	15th		1 O.R. 2/14th Batt. L.R. returned to unit	
	16th		1 mule received from mob. vet. section Weather fine Wind N.	J.T.C J.T.C
	17th		Weather fine Wind N.N.W.	
	18th		2/Lieut S.J. GURNEY reported for duty 1 O.R. 9 Draught horses 2/H.dgms 303 Brigade R.F.A returned to unit 8 O.R. 9 Draight horses 8 mules 2 H.dsgms 605 D.A.C " " Weather overcast Wind N.H. Dug out at M.34.15.b (No.2) completed Dug out at top of DOUAI (No.18) completed Bridge construction at VASE completed 12416 2. Cpl MERKEY A. evacuated from 30 C.C.S to bot LON. COY 1 O.R. 2/18th Batt L.R.A 2/24th returned to unit	J.T.C J.T.C
	19th		Weather very hot Wind N.N.H. 4 O.R. 2/4th Batt LON. REGT. att: for rations	J.T.C

WAR DIARY or INTELLIGENCE SUMMARY

Army Form C. 2118

2/4th LONDON FIELD COY R.E.

OCTOBER 1916

Place	Date	Hour	Summary of Events and Information	Remarks and references to Appendices
MARŒUIL	20th		Weather fine	D.T.C
			1 O.R 2/15th Batt Lon Regt returned to unit	
			Shoring stump pits at RHINE SHELTERS completed	
			128th Cpl GOLDSWORTHY R. Evacuated to 4/2 C.C. Stn Sund E	
			Weather fine Sund E	
	21st		H.O.R 2/15 Dug out at N.#3 (NO 19) Completed	D.T.C
			VISTULA Railway Extension Completed	
			Bridge Construction at ANNIVERSAIRE Completed	
			1 O.R 2/13th Batt L.R returned to unit	
			8 O.R 2/14th " " " "	
			4 O.R 2/15th " " " "	
			10 O.R 2/16th " " " "	
			11 D.R. 15 L.Mules, 1 Rider 116th Lon. Fld. Co. R.E. returned to unit	
			24 O.R 13 Hagra. 52 Draught Horses, 2 Riders 60th D.A.C returned to unit	
			3 O.R 4 draught Horses and 1 Hagon 302 Bde R.F.A. to unit	
			1 O.R 301 Bde R.F.A returned to unit	
			1 O.R Attd to M.M.P to unit also 2 GENDARMES	
			844 Sergt OUTRED A.W. reported on conclusion of duty at Brats Consolidation School at AGNIERS.	
			CAPT H.G. FERGUSON reported sick to hospital	

OCTOBER 1916.

WAR DIARY 2/4th LONDON FIELD COY RE

INTELLIGENCE SUMMARY

Army Form C. 2118

(Erase heading not required.)

Place	Date	Hour	Summary of Events and Information	Remarks and references to Appendices
MARŒUIL	21st		2 Lieutenants 1 O.R attached M.M.P. To unit	JXC
	22nd		Received 149th Infantry Brigade Operation Orders No 19 dated 20th dealing with handing over. Received 60th Div Eng Orders No 2 re. handing over. Weather fine Wind S.E.	JXC
	23rd		13 O.R. 1 H Wagon 2 wheels, 1 Ruler attached to rations 1393 Driver Everest A.E, 1 Maltese cart and draught horse attached from 60th Div Eng H.Q Advance Party of 9th Canadian Field Coy R.E. arrived Weather overcast Wind S.	JXC
			1 Rider loaned to 1/6th Lon Fld Coy R.E Lieut B F Nell 1/6th Lon Fld Coy R.E and 2746 Driver Jannaway (Batman) also (1 Horse Ryder) attached for duty and rations O.C 9th Canadian Field Coy R.E. was shown around the line also the works at MARŒUIL	JXC
	24th		Weather Wet II Lieut W C P Dawson 302nd Bde R.F.A. To unit	JXC

WAR DIARY 2/4th LONDON FIELD COY R.E.
INTELLIGENCE SUMMARY

OCTOBER 1916 — Army Form C. 2118

Place	Date	Hour	Summary of Events and Information	Remarks and references to Appendices
MARŒUIL	24th	8 AM	Company relieved by 9th CANADIAN FIELD COY R.E. Company left for FERME DOFFINÉ. Travelling via HAUTE AVESNES, HERMAVILLE, and TILLOY. Map Reference LENS 11 1/40,000 Arrived 12.55 P.M. Weather wet.	OTC
FERME DOFFINÉ	25th	10 AM	Company left for BUNEVILLE, travelling via ANBRINES and HOUVIN Map ref. LENS 11 1/40,000 Arrived 3.30 P.M. 2378 Sapper RADMALL T.C. 1298 Sapper PRIEST O, 3158 Sapper VICKERS A.P. 1867 Sapper LEONARD C.E. Evacuated. Received 60th DIV ENGL ORDERS No 3 and H. re move BUNEVILLE – WAVANS. Received 174th INFANTRY BRIGADE OPERATION ORDERS No 20, dealing with move BUNEVILLE – WAVANS	OTC
BUNEVILLE	26th		Weather fine. 1210 SERGT GARNER A.M. 1190 II CPL PELLS P.C. 3459 SAPPER PUGSLEY J. 3160 SAPPER CRISP A.J. Evacuated. 2446 DRIVER TANNAWAY N. 116th LONDON FIELD COY R.E. Also 1 Horse rider, returned to 116th LON FLD COY R.E. Rider returned from 1/16th LON FLD COY R.E.	OTC

1875 Wt. W593/826 1,000,000 4/15 J.B.C. & A. A.D.S.S./Forms/C.2118.

OCTOBER 1916

WAR DIARY 2/4TH LONDON FIELD COY R.E.

INTELLIGENCE SUMMARY
(Erase heading not required.)

Army Form C. 2118

Instructions regarding War Diaries and Intelligence Summaries are contained in F.S. Regs., Part II. and the Staff Manual respectively. Title Pages will be prepared in manuscript.

Place	Date	Hour	Summary of Events and Information	Remarks and references to Appendices
BUNEVILLE	Oct 28th		Weather Dull. Received 149th INFANTRY BRIGADE OPERATION ORDERS NO 21. 1 Horse (rider) relieved from MOB VET SECTION. 1284 CPL. GOLDSWORTHY R. reported from H2. B.B. Stn. 1867 SAPPER LEONARD C.E. reported	PTC
	29th		Weather Wet	PTC
		P.M. 8 H5	Company moved to WAVANS travelling via PREVENT VACQUERIE and road junction ½ mile West of M in MAMOUR F.M. Ref LENS 11 1/100,000 arrived 3:25 P.M. 3149 SAPPER MORLEY R.E. evacuated, also 1738 SAPPER ROBERTS E.W. Weather Wet	
WAVANS	29th	9 A.M.	Company moved to PROUVILLE travelling via ST. AUCHEUL and MONTIGNY Ref LENS 11 1/100,000 arrived 1.40 P.M. 1349 DRIVER CHURCHLEY evacuated Weather Wet.	PTC
PROUVILLE	30th		Company moved to TOUTENCOURT travelling via BERNAVILLE, CANDAS, LE VAL DE MAISON and PUCHEVILLERS. Ref LENS 11 1/100,000 arrived as follows P.T.O.	PTC

OCTOBER 1916.

WAR DIARY 2/4TH LONDON FIELD COY R.E.

INTELLIGENCE SUMMARY

Army Form C. 2118

Place	Date	Hour	Summary of Events and Information	Remarks and references to Appendices
PROUVILLE	30th	4.30AM 8.30AM 10.30AM	Transport arrived 3.50 P.M. Cyclists arrived 2.30 P.M. Sappers in motor lorries 1.30 P.M. Weather fine Company employed on General Repairs and roads under C.E. RESERVE ARMY HEADQUARTERS	JTC
TOUTENCOURT	31st			JTC

A.J.Culver
O.C. 2/4TH LONDON FIELD COY R.E.
MAJOR RE(T)

WAR DIARY

2/4th LONDON FIELD COY R.E.

NOVEMBER 1916

Vol 6

WAR DIARY or INTELLIGENCE SUMMARY

Army Form C. 2118

2/4th LONDON FIELD COY R.E.

NOVEMBER 1916

Place	Date	Hour	Summary of Events and Information	Remarks and references to Appendices
FONTIENCOURT	NOV 1st		Weather wet	W.F.C.
			Company left for PROVILLE as follows	
		4.30 AM	Transport arrived H.O.P.M.	
		4.30 AM	Cyclists	
			11.15 AM	
		8.0 AM	Sappers and horses arrived 11.30 AM	
PROVILLE	2nd		Weather Wet, fine later	J.F.C.
			1349 Driver CHURCHLEY W.G. reported	
			3150 Sapper CRISP A.J. reported	
			Received copy of No 8. 149th Infantry Brigade Operation Order No 23	
	3rd		Weather fine	W.F.C.
			Company moved to EAUCOURT travelling via LONGUEVILLERS, COULONVILLERS	
			ST. RIQUIER and PONT REMY	
EAUCOURT	4th		Weather Dull and Showery	W.F.C.
			The following N.C.O men reported for duty 539 SERGT JULLIEN N.E. 1938 SAPPER ROBERTS H.	
			1298 SAPPER PRIEST O. 2258 SAPPER RADNALL T. 3685 SAPPER VICKERS A.P.	
	5th		Weather Dull & Showery	W.F.C.
			Eleven O.R. detached to XV Corps for duty and rations	

WAR DIARY
INTELLIGENCE SUMMARY

2/4th LONDON FIELD COY R.E. Army Form C. 2118

NOVEMBER 1916

Place	Date	Hour	Summary of Events and Information	Remarks and references to Appendices
EAUCOURT	6th		Weather Dull Showery.	W.Y.C.
			Transfer of Lieut. B.F. NELL from 1/1st LONDON FIELD COY R.E. to 2/4th LONDON FIELD COY R.E. Published in 60th DIV ENGR R.O. No 32 to date from 21st. Authority D.H.Q. letter A/139/60/283 dated 6/11/16	
	7th		Weather Dull Some rain	W.Y.C.
			Eleven O.R. returned from XV Corps	
			CAPT. P.N. HARDCASTLE, 1393 DR. EVEREST. A.E., MALTESE CART, 1 Ride and 1 Draught returned to DIV. ENG. HQ.	
			1 Limbered Wagon G.S. and 2 draught horses handed over to A.S.C	
			1 Wagon and 2 draught horses attached from A.S.C	
			30 Bicycles handed over to D.A.D.O.S	
			Weather Dull & Showery.	W.Y.C.
	8th		31143 SAPPER MORLEY A.E. reported for duty 1783 SAPPER STEPHENSON N attached to DIV ENG HQ	
			1284 CPL GOLDSWORTHY R promoted A/Sergt } made to complete
			1920 L.CPL EATWELL N " A/Sergt } New Est. PART XII
			1350 2/CPL COLLINS J.O " A/Corpl. }
			1425 L.CPL (unpaid) BARNES C.W " A/Corpl }

NOVEMBER 1916.

WAR DIARY 2/4th LONDON FIELD COY. R.E.
INTELLIGENCE SUMMARY

Army Form C. 2118

Place	Date	Hour	Summary of Events and Information	Remarks and references to Appendices
FAUCOURT	8th		1800 SAPPER FEVYER E.N. appointed Lance Corporal	W.Y.C.
			3715 " NEWMAN. C.E. "	
			1616 DRIVER BROWN. A.E. "	
			1893 " CLAWSON. H. " { made to complete	
			1864 " RAINE. C.F. " { Army Est. Part XII	
			The following vehicles surplus to War Est Part XII were handed to D.A.D.S.	
			Wagons G.S. 1, cart's Food R.E. 8, Hagons Limbered R.E. 2	
			Weather Dull	
	9th		50 Horses taken to No2 Coy. A.S.C. Sir Trim at BELLANCOURT and exchanged for mules.	W.Y.C.
			First Inoculation of Coy. with T.A.B. completed.	
			3168. S/S HOOPER E. promoted Corporal	
			Weather Dull	
	10th		30 Surplus mules and Harness returned to No2 Coy A.S.C.	W.Y.C.
			4 Riders received from No2 Coy A.S.C.	
			Small Box Respirators received from D.A.D.O.S.	
			31 Drivers joined Coy. from No4 GENERAL BASE DEPOT.	

WAR DIARY

2/4th LONDON FIELD COY. R.E.

NOVEMBER 1916

Army Form C. 2118

Place	Date	Hour	Summary of Events and Information	Remarks and references to Appendices
EAUCOURT	10th		2/116 Driver JANNANAY W. transferred from 1/6th LONDON FIELD COY RE to H.Q.R.E. SAUNDERS V. 1804. Weather Dull	
"	11th		9 Drivers and 4 Sappers joined from Base Depot. All horses and Mules in Company Malleined. Weather Dull	
"	12th		Water Cart No E83369. 1 handed over to OC No1 Coy A.S.C. Section A.M.T.O. Weather Dull	
"	13th		Pair of Hoke Cart horses returned to No 2 Coy A.S.C.	
		7.30 P.M.	1198. CPL MEAD. H.J. reported for duty, from Base Training Camp ROUEN. Attached from 3/8th LONDON FIELD COY. RE. to H.Q.R.E. 15 Drivers, 2 pontoon wagons 1 Trestle Wagon, 2 limbered R.E. Wagons, 30 mules. Attached from 1/6th LONDON FIELD COY RE to H.Q.R.E. 15 drivers, 2 pontoon wagons 1 Trestle Wagon, 2 limbered R.E. Wagons, 30 mules. All surplus stores etc. returned to D.A.D.O.S. and Salvage Company Received copy No 8 of 149th Infantry Brigade Operation Orders No 24.	

NOVEMBER 1916.

WAR DIARY
or
INTELLIGENCE SUMMARY

2/1st LONDON FIELD COY RE Army Form C. 2118

Place	Date	Hour	Summary of Events and Information	Remarks and references to Appendices
EAUCOURT	14th		Weather Dull. The following attached from H.Q.R.E reported to the 1/6th LONDON FIELD COY R.E to position Indicators. 3 Trestle Wagons, 6 Limbered R.E Wagons, 92 mules. The following Officers and N.C.O reported to Brigade Hd Qrs. 2 LT A F NEAL, 2 LT F C PLUMB, 2 LT J E CHARNLEY, 2 LT S J GURNEY, 2 LT N B DATE, 12.12, C.Q.M.S WHAMOND. G.R. 3 Bicycles handed over to D.A.D.O.S.	J.F.C
		5.30PM	Company left for LONGPRE and entrained for MARSEILLES	
LONGPRE	15th	8.20AM	Train departed	
	16th	11.0PM	Train stopped at MACON for 1 hour	J.F.C
MARSEILLES	17th	10.AM	Train arrived MARSEILLES	J.F.C
		12.30PM	Company left for CARCASSON REST CAMP except for LT A F WILLIAMS and 37 O.R. who proceeded to FOURNIER CAMP	J.F.C
			Weather wet	
CARCASSON CAMP	18th			J.F.C
	19th	1.0PM	5 Officers and 210 O.R left CARCASSON CAMP and embarked on H.M.T "TRANSYLVANIA"	J.F.C
H.M.T TRANSYLVANIA	20th		At Sea	J.F.C
"	21st		At Sea	J.F.C

WAR DIARY 2]/4th LONDON FIELD COY R.E.
or
INTELLIGENCE SUMMARY

Army Form C. 2118

NOVEMBER 1916

Place	Date	Hour	Summary of Events and Information	Remarks and references to Appendices
H.M.T TRANSYLVANIA	22nd	12 Noon	Arrived at ST. PAUL'S BAY MALTA	WYC
MARSEILLES	"	10 AM	LT R F WILLIAMS and 19 O.R. Embarked on H.M.T "MENONINEE"	WYC
"	"		2390 DRIVER GREGORY. T evacuated to MARSEILLES STATIONERY HOSPITAL	WYC
H.M.T TRANSYLVANIA	23rd		Lying in ST. PAUL'S BAY MALTA	WYC
"	24th		Put into Port VALETTA MALTA	WYC
"	25th		Ditto	WYC
"	26th		Ditto	WYC
"	27th	10 AM	Left MALTA	WYC
"	28th		At sea	WYC
"	29th		At sea	WYC
"	30th	10 AM	Arrived "SALONIKA"	WYC
		3 PM	5 Officers 208 O.R. disembarked and marched to Rest Camp	WYC

WYCulum MAJOR. REID.
O.C. 2]/4th LONDON FIELD COY R.E.

www.ingramcontent.com/pod-product-compliance
Lightning Source LLC
Chambersburg PA
CBHW081447160426
43193CB00013B/2403